New Bar and Club Design

Bethan Ryder

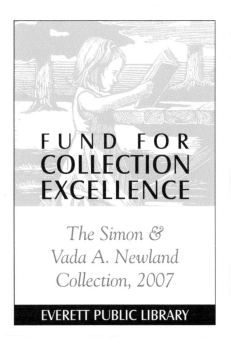

Front cover image: Kabaret's Prophecy, London
(photo: Fredrika Lökholm and Martin Slivka). With special thanks
to Kabaret's Prophecy and to UVA for on-screen title design.

Back cover image: Mirrorball at Shaun + Joe, London (photo:
Fredrika Lökholm and Martin Slivka). With thanks to Shaun + Joe.

First published in the United States of America in 2005
by Abbeville Press, 137 Varick Street, Suite 504, New York,
NY 10013.

First published in Great Britain in 2005 by Laurence King
Publishing Ltd, 71 Great Russell Street, London, WC1B 3BP

First Edition
10 9 8 7 6 5 4 3 2 1

Library of Congress Cataloging-in-Publication Data

Ryder, Bethan.
  New bar and club design / by Bethan Ryder.-- 1st ed.
    p. cm.
  Includes index.
  ISBN 0-7892-0845-8
  1. Bars (Drinking establishments)—Decoration. 2. Interior
decoration—History—21st century. 3. Interior architecture—
History—21st century. I. Title.

NK2195.R4R9323 2005
747'.8572—dc22
                          2005007024

Hardcover ISBN 0-7892-0845-8
Paperback ISBN 0-7892-0860-1

Printed in China

Designed by Plan-B Studio

Special photography (pages 18, 50, 98, 112) by Fredrika Lökholm
and Martin Slivka

Image on page 4: Loungelover, London

For bulk and premium sales and for text adoption procedures,
write to Customer Service Manager, Abbeville Press, Inc.,
137 Varick Street, New York, NY 10013 or call 1-800-ARTBOOK.

New Bar and Club Design

Bethan Ryder

Abbeville Press Publishers
New York   London

Contents

Introduction

The introduction to the first *Bar and Club Design* book traced the history of nocturnal venues, explaining how they originated from the travellers' inns and taverns of centuries ago, evolving into the slick, designer destinations of the late twentieth century. It claimed: 'Twenty years ago, a book on bar and club design would not have been possible; there simply weren't enough venues to warrant such a specific focus. Now it's the year 2001, and every city in the developed world has more than enough bars and clubs to call their own.' Four years later, the trend for operators, architects and designers continually to up the design ante in their creation of after-dark wonderlands continues apace.

In these 'lifestyle'-obsessed times, bars and clubs have become destination spaces where the modern-day *flâneur* plays out his or her public identity. Exceeding their original function of refreshment stop, they have become places of entertainment, spectacle and display. Designer bars and clubs are theatrical spaces that encourage performance; they are about leaving the quotidian behind and escaping into an exciting new realm, full of anticipation. Who knows what the night ahead might hold in store?

Like its predecessor, *New Bar and Club Design* is a showcase of projects from around the globe, chosen for their beauty, uniqueness, downright weirdness or the innovation of their design. They are 'styled' and contrived environments, rather than simply places to drink or dance. As stated before, the shelf-life of a bar or club is generally shorter than that of other commercial leisure establishments, and, therefore, such venues are more likely to be inspired by the whims of fashion, with designers willing to experiment and push the boundaries in terms of materials and themes. All the projects in this book were completed since the publication of *Bar and Club Design*, and, as a group, they represent the design *Zeitgeist* of hedonistic venues in the early 'Noughties'.

This book is organized into four chapters: Bars, Restaurant Bars, Hotel Bars and Clubs. (The particular histories of these bar types were given in *Bar and Club Design.*) These categories are not wholly definitive; they simply serve as a practical guide for architects and designers wishing to examine a specific kind of bar. Indeed, over the past four years, the boundaries between types of establishment have become increasingly blurred, with restaurants and hotel bars often morphing into clubs (with DJs and dancing) later in the evening, and many new nightclubs including clearly defined dining areas. Each project has been placed in the chapter that best describes its *primary* function.

above
The Blue Bar at London's Berkeley Hotel, where David Collins has combined classical Lutyens details with contemporary design.

opposite
Fabio Novembre's Café L'Atlantique in Milan, with its shimmering cascade of fibre-optics, has survived a decade.

In *Bar and Club Design*, several elements were identified as the main preoccupations of bar and club designers at the end of the twentieth century. In providing nocturnal arenas for the pursuit of pleasure, designers were offering several things to attract and seduce patrons: comfort, escapism, flexibility and theatricality. These basics tenets were expressed via various themes and aesthetics, with several clear trends emerging, such as a return to nature, global influences, nostalgia for the past and retro-futurism.

Since then, we've entered a bewildering age of uncertainty, which in many ways seems to have reinforced the human desire to socialize, party, forget our sorrows and, if possible, leave the horrors of the world behind; as the old expression goes, fiddling while Rome burns. And so, rather than there being a new world order when it comes to bar and club design, many of these trends have been reinforced in the early twenty-first century. Perhaps it is because they are borne of eternal human interests: a love of the world around us (nature), an obsession with 'other' life-forms (space-age retro-futurism), a tendency to seek solace in the familiar past (heritage and vintage influences) and a fascination with other cultures (Japanese or Moroccan themes, for example). After all, most designers take their inspiration from things that surround them.

Beyond these preoccupations, the most interesting developments in bar and club design have been in technology; progressive computer programmes, construction methods, lighting and materials have all enabled architects and designers to achieve their dreams in methods never seen before. Thanks to the inexorable march of technology, the bar essentials of comfort, flexibility, theatricality and escapism are being offered in thrilling new ways.

left
Icebergs in Sydney's Bondi Beach, by Lazzarini Pickering, features a palette of greens and blues inspired by the ocean below.

above
The Absolute IceBar Milano in The Town House 12 Hotel was modelled on the original in Jukkasjärvi in Sweden and built using ice from the Torne river.

opposite left
The Plettenberg Bay Hotel's Sandbar, designed by Hot Cocoa, uses rough sand-like surfaces, rope tables and seaside photography inspired by the surrounding South African beaches.

opposite right
Bernard Khoury's rooftop bar at Centrale restaurant in Beirut allows patrons the romance of drinking beneath the stars.

Organic forms

Nature continues to be a great source of inspiration, as many of the projects in this book demonstrate. An extreme example is the Absolut Vodka-sponsored Icebar, constructed from pure ice. Its creators have taken the igloo-inspired concept (which originated in Lapland) abroad, and there is now a permanent Icebar in Milan, Italy. On a slightly more subtle level, Lazzarini Pickering Architects incorporated ocean blues and aquamarines when designing their restaurant and bar Icebergs, overlooking Bondi Beach in Sydney. Jordan Mozer's Nectar was also inspired by the cool hues and fluidity of 'melted ice', to form a contrast to the 'cooked' textures and palette of the adjoining restaurant (see page 58).

Trends are cyclical, however, and designers appear to be less interested in water-related themes or features as they were a few years ago. Whether it forms part of a desire for greater security in the present world climate, or is just a trickling down of Frank Gehry's 'Bilbao effect', the current obsession in bar and club design across the globe is with cocoons, or cave-like structures, and amoebic shapes. Curvaceous, organic forms are *de rigueur*, and, paradoxically, made increasingly possible to construct via modern technology. There are almost two strands here: those that appear as quite primitive forms, as if hewn from the rock itself, and others that are like more perfectly hatched ovoid capsules, as if beamed down from outer space.

Pioneering examples of this latter trend are Jakob + MacFarlane's silver-lined cloud-like caves, which give Georges, at the top of the Pompidou Centre in Paris, its undulating landscape, and the white lunarscape of Sketch's East Bar, with its satellite pod toilets, in London. Leo A. Daly and Adam D. Tihany's new Teatro Bar in Las Vegas exhibits an ovoid form almost identical to that of the East Bar at Sketch. Like a grounded flying saucer, it operates as a self-contained bar capsule in the larger space of the MGM Grand Casino. The cocoon is taken to its extreme at the CocoonClub in Frankfurt (see page 168).

Designed by 3deluxe, this vast superclub has a DJ booth that resembles a hovering alien craft, and 'membrane' walls surrounding the dance floor contain lurid green seating 'cocoons', where guests can recline and take a break from dancing.

In the more organic, earthy vein is Andy Martin Associates' Opal in London, a subterranean, craggy cavern of a bar, inspired by César Manrique's 1970s lava-rock creations on the island of Lanzarote (see page 32). Juan Carlos Arcila-Duque's redesign of MYNT in Miami includes a rock-like sculptural entrance, albeit lacquered to create a glossy effect (see page 40).

Zokei Syudan's Yusaku Kaneshiro often incorporates cave formations into his projects, inspired by his native island of Okinawa. Both So-An and Ashibina in Tokyo contain enclosures more typically found in nature, the former a booth constructed from twigs and the latter a series of actual caves (see pages 28 and 74). Despite its disco lighting, Stephane Dupoux's New York boutique club Cielo can also be considered part of this movement (see page 132). Its log-lined interior provides comfort, while creating a back-to-nature security like that of a rural mountain cabin.

On a larger, more impressive scale, the Malaysian mega-club Zouk has a distinctive, whitewashed stucco exterior informed by vernacular adobe architecture and bulbous organic forms (see page 152). The rather more refined restaurant and bar Zenzibar in Shanghai has an internal cocoon structure fabricated from slatted timber, which contains dining booths, effectively separating the bar from restaurant (see page 78). Most dramatic of the more rustic organic forms, however, is the Coconclub in Moscow (sadly damaged by fire at the time of writing and no longer open), which rises up inside its host building, like a giant termite mound (see page 160). Formed from plywood, it is sanded so smoothly that it resembles stratified rock, eroded by the sea. Like Sketch, it even has its own satellite toilet pod, elevated on a single column and attached to the main bar space by a small glass walkway.

Rustic textures

Often attending the use of organic forms is a predilection on the part of designers for rural, natural materials and textures. Stephane Dupoux's New York boutique club Quo was inspired by 'Urban Tropicalism' and features cobblestone walls and perspex bars containing sand (see page 178). In Gstaad, Switzerland, Patrick Jouin took his influences from Le Chlösterli's ancient farmyard heritage and employed stone paving more typically used outdoors for the venue's floor and table tops (see page 92). In London, rough, textured walls are all part of the 1960s Spanish-cave vibe of Opal, and Kuala Lumpur's Zouk features adobe and cracked mosaic surfaces.

Elsewhere, natural textures are strongly evoked, such as at Andy Martin Associates' Villa Zévaco in Casablanca, where the terrazzo floors of the Library bar are smooth and monochrome, but designed to resemble pebbles (see page 84). Super Potato's love of natural materials, in particular timber, is abundantly clear at Shochu Lounge in London, where the bar counter is a thick slab of ancient elm, roughly hewn to reveal its natural state (see page 96). Even the rather slick Universum Lounge in Berlin has pebble-dashed wall finishes, presumably inspired by the rough surface of the moon (see page 20). Meanwhile, on the west coast of America, Jorge Pardo's Mountain is enriched by a soil-like, brown, acoustical spray that covers the ceiling and by the dark-brown, liquid drips that adorn the wood-panelled walls (see page 24).

above left
Beamed down from outer-space: the West Bar in London's Sketch.

above
Patrick Jouin's bar at Alain Ducasse's Mix restaurant at the Mandalay Bay Casino, Las Vegas, displays organic influences in the branch-like structure above the bar.

opposite top
Wrapped up in stripes: the bar at the Dream Hotel in New York.

opposite left
A flamboyant floral window transfer provides some privacy at Point 101 bar in London, by bar-and-club designer Shaun Clarkson.

opposite right
Inside Point 101 fibre-optic chandeliers add decadence and glamour.

Rich pattern

Just as texture is being explored, so, too, is pattern. Designers are definitely on the rebound from plain, minimal interiors, or the bleached, 'white canvas' venues popular in recent years. They are embracing pattern with relish. In some cases, this can be viewed as a form of nostalgia, and, again, is often inspired by nature. Just as Art Nouveau made use of modern materials in its day to produce architecture that represented floral and fauna, today designers are using CAD, laser-cutting and mosaic to create decorative walls, patterned screens and other surfaces bearing motifs drawn from nature.

Some examples of this are ordered and geometric, such as Edward van Vliet's Japanese-influenced, back-lit screens at Hotel Derlon (see page 110), the floral, hexagonal wall tiles at Zenzibar and the tiles arranged in a 'fish-scale' pattern at Zouk. Other projects feature flamboyant and baroque elements, such as Gatserelia Design's Crystal in Beirut, with its florid iron- and plasterwork (see page 56), the Helsinki Club, with its madly swirling carpeted lounge (see page 126), and the decadent Swarovski crystal-studded design of the bar at Kabaret's Prophecy in London, its pattern echoed in the leather of the booth seating (see page 142).

Guests in the bar at Florence's UNA Hotel Vittoria can gaze out at a looping mosaic 'carpet' of flowers, designed by Fabio Novembre (see page 104). Flowers also feature in the vast wall murals of the CocoonClub's InBetween Lounge. Further east, in Tokyo, Zokei Syudan gave So-An a tropical 'flower and grass' theme, manifest in the decorative pattern of Japanese paper on the ceiling (see page 28). Meanwhile, in Sydney, guests of The Loft, designed by Dale Jones-Evans, are immersed in warm, glowing foliage, created by the walls and ceiling of back-lit, laser-cut plywood screens (see page 68).

Developments in computer-programmed LEDs and other forms of lighting have encouraged designers to use light as decoration more than ever before. Although nature remains a source of inspiration in decoration and pattern-making, so does technology itself. This is most clearly identifiable in the club category, where operators are keen to create entire 'other worlds' to impress the twenty-first century's discerning, globetrotting clubbers. Here, designers are creating futuristic interiors more like computer screens or sci-fi film sets than anything else. Electronic patterns are executed most dramatically in London at the David Collins-designed Kabaret's Prophecy, with its ever-mutating, 'blinging' disco walls, in Amsterdam with Jimmy Woo's dance-floor canopy of lightbulbs (see page 118), and in the Tron-like, LED-grid interior of São Paulo's club D-Edge (see page 150).

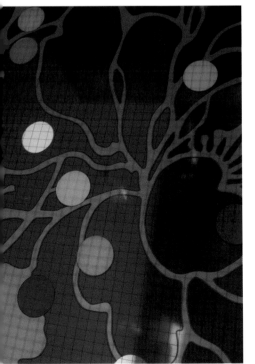

below left
Spin right round on the
glowing record dance-floor
of Nirvana's basement club
in Paris.

below right
The bar at Blue Fin in New
York's Times Square is
bright with internally
illuminated drink stands.

opposite
Philippe Starck's bar at
Ian Schrager's Hudson
Hotel feels like a futuristic
film set.

Light Fantastic

This leads us to consider lighting more
generally. Judging by many of the projects in
this book, the halcyon days of disco are back in
rainbow-hued abundance. One of the first bars to
revive a *Saturday Night Fever* floor was Brit-art
dealer Gavin Brown's Passerby, which adjoined his
hip, downtown art gallery in Manhattan. Artist Piotr
Uklanski's multi-coloured, illuminated dance floor
set a trend back in 1998, which Philippe Starck and
Ian Schrager followed with the glowing floor at the
Hudson hotel bar.

Since then, lighting has become an integral
part of the structure of many bar and club interiors.
Tripping the light fantastic is straightforward today
it seems; you simply have to step across the
threshold. Following the under-lit principle of
Passerby and the Hudson is Jimmy Woo in
Amsterdam, which features illuminated seating
platforms. Le Chlösterli has a dance floor with
bottom-lit paving stones that change colour (see
page 93), and New York club Avalon by Desgrippes
Gobé Group has internally lit, frosted-acrylic paving,
guiding patrons to its door (see page 134). Inside,
Avalon's unisex toilets are like light installations –
cubes of aluminium-framed, honeycomb Panelite,
back-lit with fluorescents to glow white and attract
clubbers. Light also provides drama at MYNT in
Miami, XL in New York (see page 46), Zenzibar
in Shanghai, The Loft in Sydney, 747 in Sicily (see
page 86) and Hotel Derlon in Maastricht, in the
form of back-lit opaque walls or screens. These
elements occasionally conceal digitally
programmed neon or LED lighting, which changes
colour and thus alters the mood of an interior.

At other venues, lighting has been used
more structurally. At Glamorous's Hajime and Drop
Kick in Tokyo (see pages 88 and 30), internally lit
elements define the layout.

GRAFT installed acid-etched glass in the gaps formed by their red 'cradle-like' structure, and back-lit these to emphasize the sculptural quality of the Q! Hotel bar in Berlin, and to reinforce the lack of traditional walls, ceiling or floor (see page 106). Lighting is part of the furniture at Derlon, where the cocktail tables are illuminated cubes. In New York, the Reed Room of crobar is lit by floor-to-ceiling resin 'reeds' (see page 140), and the first bar at Helsinki Club is bathed in variously coloured lighting. A similar technique is used throughout Karim Rashid's Powder to create an ethereal effect and mutability of space (see page 180).

Exploiting the phototropic nature of humans, designers are also making the actual bars themselves the central glowing attraction of venues. The tempered-glass bar at So-An radiates a green light, the *liuli* bar at TMSK in Shanghai shines a riot of rainbow colours (see page 82), and L.A. Design's perspex cockpit bar at 747 contains gel-wrapped, fluorescent tubes that change hue and intensity. Andy Wahloo is built from decorative bricks, backed by orange perspex, which is back-lit, and the bars at Avalon emit a golden warmth, produced by back-lit parchment paper.

Most exciting and progressive of all are the kaleidoscopic, audio-synchronized lighting systems installed at Cielo, Kabaret's Prophecy, Quo, Jimmy Woo and D-Edge. You could say that today's designers are light years ahead of the rest of us, playing with technology to create throbbing walls of sound and light to dazzle clubbers around the globe.

Global hybrids

Bar and Club Design documented the popularity of Moroccan-, Russian- and Asian-themed interiors. Designers remain inspired by other cultures, but are increasingly blending them with various global elements or interpreting these influences in more subtle forms. Jonathan Amar's Nirvana restaurant and bar in Paris is a kitsch trip and psychedelic homage to India, full of mosaic, colours, twinkling LED lighting and other decoration (see *Restaurant Design*).

Indeed, the East continues to fascinate designers of bars in the West; Philippe Starck's Kong is based on a cross-pollination of Japanese and European styles (see page 52). Edward van Vliet's Derlon is partly inspired by Japanese design, as is ViBE in Athens. Casper Reinders's Jimmy Woo is modelled on the home of a Chinese Hong Kong businessman who likes to throw parties, and is full of Chinese and Japanese antiques, artworks and other artefacts. The Japanese designers of both Shochu and Megu (see page 60) are exporting a taste of Japan to London and New York respectively. Most unique is Andy Wahloo by artist Hassan Hajjij, which, a little like Kong, is a cultural hybrid, this time combining Moroccan influences with western design to inventive effect.

Recycled elements

There are some examples of the innovative recycling of objects, whether inspired by the influential Droog Design, or simply a case of resourcefulness. The canopy above the bar at Red Cat Club (see page 116) is comprised of plastic canteen trays; likewise the stunning screen at Megu, which is composed of sake bottles and rice bowls stacked on a rod. More utilitarian in aesthetic is Perbacco in Sitges, where Oriented Strand Board, usually used only temporarily in construction, forms the entire interior (see page 34). In a similar Do-It-Yourself, reclaim-and-reinvent vein, Andy Wahloo's interior is constructed from old road signs, with grocery products for decoration. In London, the implements and materials used in the distillation of the spirit shochu form much of the interior at the Shochu Lounge, and at Megu in New York, antique obi sashes enliven the ceiling and walls. Such creativity is often more common in low-budget productions, but it is evidently creeping into the more lavish projects, too.

opposite top
The Indian-inspired psychedelia of Nirvana, with its pink heart-shaped bar by Jonathan Amar.

opposite bottom
Nature goes pop at Stephane Dupoux's bar at Cocoon Restaurant in London, crowned by a coral-like Ayala Serfaty light.

above
Adam D. Tihany's Agua Bar at the One&Only Palmilla resort in Los Cabos, Mexico.

Retro/Nostalgia

Architects and designers have always looked to the past for inspiration. Many projects in this book include ingredients or stylistic references to previous decades, not only the new wave of clubs that is reinventing disco, but also in other projects. Some are simply a case of circumstance: venues such as Villa Zévaco are framed by their existing host building – in this case a 1950s design. Here, the designer attempts to respect such heritage, while reinterpreting it in a twenty-first-century way. Others, such as Red Cat Club, use a hotch-potch of styles, with 1970s-style wallpaper, lampshades inspired by the 1950s, and so on, almost to confound classification.

The 1970s appear to be a popular decade, identifiable not only in the disco revival, but also in the decadence of Crystal – modelled on the club in *Scarface* – and the curved geometry and particular hues of Himmelreich (see page 54), as well as the Verner Panton-style seating of the UNA bar, the retro colours of Cielo, and the kitsch lampshades, fabrics and decoration of Andy Wahloo. The 1960s also continue to fascinate; Opal references the sets of the cult film *Barbarella*, with its caves, while Universum Lounge expresses a James-Bond-meets-the-space-race style of retro-futurism.

Trends aside, it's apparent that when it comes to nocturnal venues designers are continuing to let their imaginations run wild. Whether these bars and clubs manage to glow for a decade, or burn brightly and fizzle out after one year, they are all a weird and wonderful testament to the limitless creativity inspired by the pursuit of pleasure. This book salutes them all.

above
Teatro's dramatic interior by US design heavyweight Adam D. Tihany, at the MGM Grand in Las Vegas.

opposite
External views of Teatro reveal Leo A. Daly's futuristic flying-saucer pod structure.

Chapter One: *Bars*

Universum Lounge / Berlin, Germany

Plajer & Franz Studio, March 2001

above
Teak bar tables feature handy slot compartments for cocktail menus.

opposite
Ground Control to Major Tom: the digital clock displays Houston time.

Universum Lounge, situated in the Lehniner Platz in Charlottenburg, is the second Berlin bar project by local architects Alexander Plajer and Werner Franz. (Their first, Lounge 808 (featured in *Bar and Club Design*), is in the 'edgier' nightlife district of Mitte, in former East Germany.) The space-age concept was inspired by the host building, the Schaubühne theatre. Designed by Bauhaus architect Erich Mendelsohn in the 1920s, the landmark building was originally the Universum Cinema.

The arc-shaped layout of the Universum Lounge was dictated by the curves of the existing architecture. Although Plajer & Franz have characteristically used rich, classic 1920s materials, the forms of the interior are more retro-futuro, alluding to the space-race optimism and American lounge culture of the 1960s and early 1970s. This is, as the designers put it, 'James Bond, lost in space'.

Bespoke, white faux-leather banquettes are matched with brown-and-white tulip-based stools and chunky teak tables. The astronautical whites are anchored by the earthy tones of the wall finishes and the bar, which features a thick teak top and a geometric, bronze-plated bar façade, evocative of Bauhaus design.

Horizontally ribbed, teak wall-panelling emphasizes the sweeping arcs of the internal architecture. These curves are echoed in the lunarscape lightbox, displayed prominently on the end wall. Here, the recessed image appears like a view of the moon's surface, framed by the lozenge-shaped window of a space vehicle that has just landed. Next to this, a large digital clock, displaying Houston time, represents 'Ground Control'.

More glamorous than any interplanetary craft, the Universum Lounge is a fitting space odyssey for 2001.

10 · 16 · 88

ViBE / Athens, Greece

....

Dimitris Naoumis, January 2003

In recent years, Athens has shrugged off its historic-city
image, earned some street cred and emerged as a hip,
modern European destination, boosted substantially, of
course, by the 2004 Olympics. Today, the Greek capital boasts
a clutch of boutique hotels, and the bar and club scene is
becoming increasingly sophisticated and design-led.

ViBE bar sits in a former ruin in the nightlife hotspot
of Psiri, Athens's answer to Soho, described by one local as
'a sort of dark place that echoes its underworld past'. Local
designer Dimitris Naoumis was asked by the client to 'create
a club that would contain the simplicity of Japanese
minimalism, combined with a strong taste of New York style'.

Naoumis answered the brief by dividing the concept
in two. 'On the ground floor, the simplicity of the Japanese

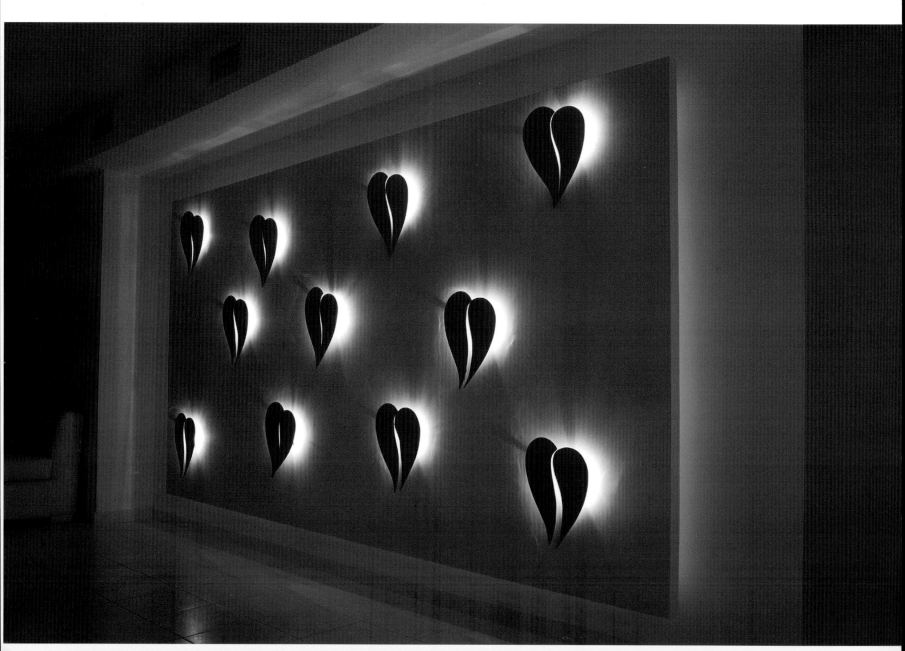

left
The sparse ground-floor bar is lit by wenge-framed papyrus lightboxes.

below left
The hallway is decorated with a Japanese-influenced red perspex and Inox mobile.

opposite
An installation of broken hearts lights the upstairs lounge at ViBE.

minimalism, in combination with the atmosphere of the neon lights, gives the place a New York character,' he says. 'The second floor is called "Future Pop", and the minimal aesthetic combines with the refreshing power of the 1960s decade and explores the "future" side of pop art.'

The ground-floor space is sparse, housing a dark wenge-wood bar, with bespoke light installations providing the only ornamentation. Behind the bar, a grid of 16 wenge-framed lighting panels, dressed with handmade original papyrus, radiate various colours and intensities. At the rear, the 5.5 metre (18 foot) double-height area is enlivened by a red perspex and Inox mobile.

Upstairs, an installation of red polycarbonide 'broken hearts' drenches the, predominantly white and red, interior in warm, orange lighting. On the opposite wall, a display of small, white square plaques echoes the papyrus panels of the ground floor. Furniture throughout was custom-designed for the project by Naoumis. As the name suggests, ViBE is a DJ bar playing a diverse mix of R'n'B, electronic, world and classical music.

Mountain / Los Angeles, USA

Jorge Pardo and Mark Manus, June 2003

opposite
Pardo's 21 lanterns will change annually to signify the new year.

below
Mountain's distinctive red façade in LA's Chinatown, an area recently colonized by artists and gallery owners.

Mountain, located in LA's Chinatown, is no ordinary bar. It is also an artwork by Californian resident Jorge Pardo. This Cuban-born artist's work challenges the conventional distinctions of art and architecture, sculpture and design. He creates environments that occupy a liminal position between the disciplines; they are thought-provoking, open-ended installations, which refuse categorization.

Pardo's most famous creation is his own private residence, '4166 Sea View Lane'. Commissioned by the Los Angeles Museum of Contemporary Art, it briefly operated as a gallery, before becoming his home. Mountain can be considered in the context of other international Pardo installations, most notably Glasgow's Centre for Contemporary Arts bar and the K2 gallery's bar and restaurant in Düsseldorf. Mountain isn't attached to an art space, but is situated in an area that has become saturated with contemporary art galleries.

The property was originally General Lee's Man Jen Low restaurant, which dates back to 1860, but moved to its present spot in 1938, when Chinatown was relocated. The 1950s and 1960s were Chinatown's glamorous heyday, but the bright lights faded in the 1970s due to suburbanization. Then, as with many neglected urban neighbourhoods, artists pioneered the subsequent gentrification by moving into the area from the late 1990s.

Jointly owned by Jorge Pardo, local art dealer and owner of China Art Objects Galleries Steve Hanson and architect Mark Manus, Mountain was created as a place for people to hang out after previews and gallery openings. Pardo took inspiration for the interior from Chinatown itself and 'the meandering path of his own art-making,' says Manus. The double-height ground floor accommodates up to 140 people; the refurbishment of the upstairs space is still in progress.

Pardo's unusual finishes and autumn-colour palette, with 'Roma tomato red' as the dominant shade, make for a wonderfully warm, richly textured interior. Custom-

Mountain

Chapter I: Bars

made, triangular ceramic floor tiles in burnt, earthy shades complement the walls of horizontally grooved, staggered red-painted plywood panels, adorned by a natural pattern of dark-brown liquid drips. Dark-brown acoustical spray lends the ceiling a rough soil-like effect.

A random constellation of 21 Pardo lanterns, in varying sizes (that will change annually to signify the new year) provide ambient lighting. The shades are fabricated from heat-formed PVC and decorated with a computer-graphic print on the exterior and hand-painted on the inside. Additional recessed ceiling spots are kept low 'to keep an intimate environment'.

The bar itself, with an overhead shelving unit, is tucked beneath the sloping mezzanine level. The shelving consists of a birch plywood frame with smoked perspex panels and a front grill of birch ply. Simple steel-based stools and banquettes are upholstered in distressed brown leather and small, wall-mounted timber tables have been designed to resemble polygonal flower shapes and painted to correspond with the floor tiles. Yellow-ochre drapes, bearing a hand-painted interpretation of the graphic motif on the lanterns, filter golden light into the bar, elevating its burnished glow.

opposite
The front grill of the overhead bar shelving bears an abstracted form of the drip pattern in walnut veneer.

So-An / Tokyo, Japan

Zokei Syudan, April 2001

So-An shochu bar is situated in the Tokyo business district of Shinbashi, on the top floor of the same seven-storey building that houses Ashibina, another Zokei Syudan-designed restaurant-bar. Situated close to Shinbashi Station, both venues are frequented by homeward-bound commuters.

Shochu liquor was once sake's poor relation, but this spirit (distilled from raw produce, such as rice or buckwheat) has experienced a renaissance in Japan, to the extent that it actually outsold sake in 2003. Fruit and herbs are added to create flavoured shochu, such as plum or lemongrass, and it is proving to be a big hit amongst women drinkers. 'The owner wanted us to create a woman-friendly shochu bar,' explains Yusaku Kaneshiro of Zokei Syudan, 'and had already decided

upon the name so we chose a feminine "grass and flower" theme for the interior.' As with Ashibina, Kaneshiro was inspired by his tropical homeland of Okinawa, and the small 58-cover venue is alive with organic materials and forms.

So-An's centrepiece is the bar itself, with its glowing counters of tempered glass. The smooth bar surface is punctuated at intervals with holes that function as vases, each designed to hold a single flower. The ceiling is decorated with Japanese paper, bearing a floral pattern, and contains a number of leaf-shaped coffers, internally lit in green to cast ghostly shadows on the bar top and other surfaces below. The leaf motif is repeated in the

illuminated, emerald- and earth-hued floor tiles, made of strengthened glass, that guide patrons through the space.

The natural theme is reinforced further by the 10-person cave, constructed from a steel-framed enclosure that is covered by a complex lattice of twigs. The cave houses a large, oval-shaped table that, again, echoes the leaf form. A glass top allows its ancient support to be seen – a gnarled piece of driftwood from a beach.

opposite left
Organic-inspired decoration features a canopy of twigs, arching up over seating.

opposite right
The tempered-glass bar glows green, in keeping with the 'grass and flowers' theme.

plan
The bar is the centrepiece of So-An, which accommodates only 58 patrons. 1. bar kitchen, 2. closed kitchen, 3. party room, 4. toilets

below
The leaf motif of the illuminated floor tiles is echoed above in the form of internally lit ceiling coffers.

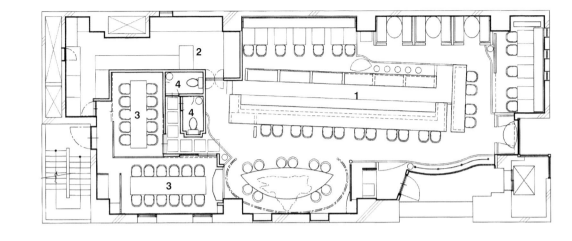

Drop Kick / Tokyo, Japan

....

Glamorous, May 2003

Suspending a giant disco glitterball outside a bar is a dazzling way of tantalizing the party crowd. It is classic Glamorous; the design firm, established in 1996 and formerly known as Morita Yasumichi Design Office, are masters in the art of exploiting the phototropic nature of humans.

'There are thousands of bars and clubs in the Roppongi neighbourhood, and so the bar needed to be very eye-catching,' explains Yasumichi Morita. 'The mirror ball is one of my favourite items and symbolic of a club, so I did something no one else has ever done and hung the ball outside.' This sparkling beacon, measuring almost 1 metre (3 feet) in diameter, is echoed by a curved wall of mirrored tiles on Drop Kick's façade. The two elements create a striking disco diptych, which frames the doorway.

Morita's desire to produce an 'alluring' interior was inspired by the sexy image of a woman's legs in fishnet tights. Internally lit, fishnet-clad columns are used to define areas within the club's space. They are made of frosted acrylic pipe, wrapped in fishnet and then encased in clear acrylic pipe, and move through changing hues of red, pink, purple and blue. The fishnet pattern is also engraved in the polished black top of the bar counter, which is lit by oil lamps.

The tiny 37 square metre (400 square foot) interior seats only 22 people and is a prime example of Glamorous's talent for creating a sense of intrigue in small spaces, through a combination of lighting and materials. Behind the glowing columns, black back-laminated glass walls create the illusion of depth, and bespoke furniture, upholstered in crocodile-skin-embossed black leather, fades into the shadows.

Two custom-made tables in the seating booths feature glitter domes, attached beneath the frosted table tops. Lit from below, they cast a halo of stars across the floor, emphasizing the glinting mirror chips, embedded in the crimson tiles. Drop Kick may lack size, but Glamorous have ensured that it sparkles from inside out.

above left
A glitterball takes pride of place on the façade, enticing guests into the club.

above
Inside, tables continue the glitterball theme, casting stars across the floor.

opposite
Fishnet-clad columns are internally lit to glow various colours.

Drop Kick

Opal / London, UK

Andy Martin Associates, September 2003

This rocky, Barbarella-esque venue lurks beneath L'Etranger restaurant in London's South Kensington. Its craggy interior was inspired by the late artist César Manrique, who, during the 1970s and 1980s, created a number of organic buildings and landscape-preservation projects, hewn from solidified lava, on the volcanic island of Lanzarote.

'Manrique discovered these molten bubble-caves in Lanzarote and built interiors inside them,' explains the creator of Opal, Australian-born architect and designer Andy Martin. 'So the whole idea was to replicate the feeling of someone's personal underground cave. I wanted to generate a Spanish 1960s hippy vibe.'

Little structural work was necessary, since the space had been a club. With a limited budget of £110,000 ($200,000), Martin constructed a basic,

utilitarian bar, with a concrete-block wall and timber top. The molten-lava effect was achieved with colour render. 'It was just thrown on and sculpted,' says Martin. 'We cut into it to create crevices and openings between areas to add interest.' The floor is painted screed, but with inlaid, dark-stained timber in places to add texture and to denote the dance floor.

Recessed lighting enhances the organic forms. Angled, low-voltage spots, set into the render, cast shafts of light, emphasizing the craggy surface textures. Other lights, inserted deep within the rock, set the alcoves aglow. 'Australia is full of caves, and there's a way they light them that's romantic and mysterious, so we're trying to recreate that feel,' says Martin.

Bespoke leather-upholstered furniture is colour-coded according to area. Banquettes surrounding the dance floor are orange, the VIP nook has grey-green accents and

another area features splashes of red. Circular tables and Pop Art-style stools, bearing an orange target motif, complete the 1960s look.

Opal is an organic work in progress. 'I'm commissioning young artists to craft things from found materials, like driftwood. Some pieces will be quite psychedelic. We might start a pottery collection to give it a sense of home, too.' Opal may appear worlds apart from Martin's slicker commercial interiors, such as Isola restaurant, also in London, but why shouldn't an antipodean designer with a surfing habit want to create a funky cave that rocks?

above
The dance floor is defined sunken timber sections, configured in a circle.

above
Craggy walls of painted plaster emulate lava rock.

right
Walk this way: fluid shapes painted on the floor guide guests to Opal.

Perbacco / Sitges, Spain

Workcelona, July 2003

Chapter I: Bars

Perbacco is a wine shop, designed to function as a wine bar in the evenings. Located in Sitges, a seaside resort not far from Barcelona, the stark simplicity of its 55 square metre (590 square foot) interior was inspired by a 'wine box without a top'. Against this honest, no-frills backdrop, the ceremony of purchasing and sampling wines takes centre stage.

Stefan Colli of Workcelona was asked to transform the former tailor's workshop on a limited budget. His solution was to use engineered wood panelling, otherwise know as Oriented Strand Board (OSB), for the floor, walls and the bar. More typically used as temporary construction board, this cheap material lends Perbacco a lo-fi, utilitarian feel. Simple, stainless-steel bar stools complete the clean, pared-down aesthetic.

Wine bottles are displayed on stainless-steel shelving and lit by concealed fluorescent lighting. The tasting table is illuminated by a Maarten van Severen lamp. There are plans to convert the basement level below into a private tasting area.

far left
Wines are displayed on utilitarian stainless-steel shelving.

below left
Engineered wood panelling, more typically used in construction, lends Perbacco its lo-fi aesthetic.

below right
The central table operates as both bar and wine-tasting counter.

Woman / Terrassa, Spain

....

Lola Lago Interiores, December 2002

above
Lago's bar design displays Memphis-style influences.

opposite
Fibre-glass legs in stockings straddle the entrance to Woman.

The colossal pair of stocking-clad legs in red stilettos that bestride the entrance, topped off by a crotch-skimming skirt, emblazoned with a pink-neon 'Woman' sign, suggests that this is a nightclub with a difference. As the saucy 6.5 metre (21 foot) high fibre-glass sculpture connotes, Woman is an 'erotic bar' for men only, combined with a brothel. It is designed, however, by a woman.

Spanish interior designer Lola Lago admits she found the refurbishment project a challenge. 'It surprises me, but in essence one tries to adapt oneself to an activity as old as the world itself, to the approaches of a modern society going towards the twenty-first century.'

The 500 square metre (1,640 square foot) venue is located in a neighbourhood full of warehouses, in the industrial town of Terrassa, not far from Barcelona. The bar takes up most of the ground floor, while, upstairs, 12 themed bedrooms accommodate the girls and their clients. 'The execution took about one year,' says Lago, 'in which the love and hate for the task appeared and disappeared constantly. It has been complex and intense, but the result answers the brief: an intimate locale, where the clients can not only use the rooms, but also get themselves a drink.'

Woman

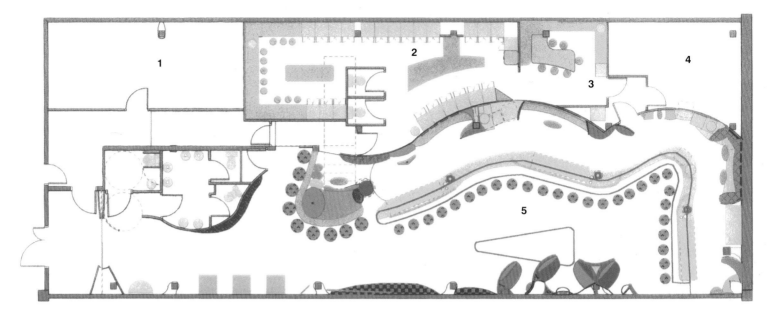

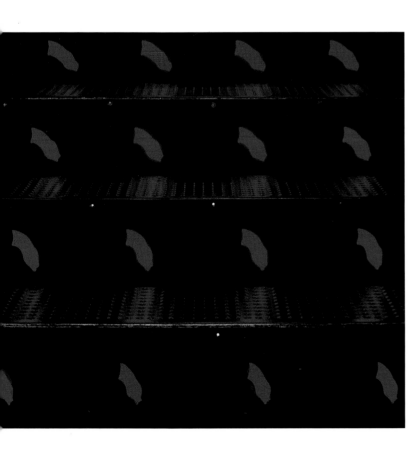

plan
The bar occupies most of the 250 square metre (820 square foot) ground floor. 1. jacuzzi, 2. cloakroom, 3. dining area, 4. store, 5. bar

opposite
Each of the 12 bedrooms is themed; pictured here is the cerise 'Madonna' room.

below
Back-illuminated phallus motifs on stair treads grow more erect as clients ascend the stairs to the bedrooms.

Lago treated the project as 'a black box, in which the illumination has to be very detailed and indirect, and in which furniture creates sculptures, which will give proper style to the interiors.' Elements of the bar interior – the abstract bar façade, splashes of bright, elemental colours set against a black background, plus the eclectic combination of materials – render it a twenty-first-century reincarnation of the radical 1980s Memphis Group style, which Lago acknowledges.

Throughout the scheme, Lago has made various visual puns, from the pop-art-style entrance, which includes paving that depicts a pair of breasts with spotlights for nipples, to the internal stairs, where each tread is illuminated by phallus motifs, back-lit to glow red. As clients ascend, they are guided by these 'members', which slowly grow, becoming fully erect on the higher steps. 'I created continuous allusions, because I wanted to have fun planning the project,' explains Lago.

Guest rooms (all en suite) are equally tongue-in-cheek, with each of them inspired by iconic women and loosely themed to 'pass through the different twentieth-century styles'. 'Lewinsky' is decorated as a small American loft, with a sofa masquerading as a pair of red lips; 'Marilyn' is 1950s-style, with heart motifs; 'Cicciolina' has a 1980s Italian décor; and 'Madonna' has a bright-cerise, round bed and red bathroom tiling, featuring a holy cross. Woman may not be to everyone's taste, particularly in terms of concept and purpose, but it is certainly a novel design solution to an ancient profession.

MYNT / Miami, USA

A-D, November 2003

MYNT was an overnight success when it opened in 2001 in Miami's hip South Beach area. Local interior and furniture designer Juan Carlos Arcila-Duque was given 'absolute freedom' to create a classic lounge on a site that had lain abandoned for almost a decade. During the 1950s, it housed one of Miami Beach's most famous hang-outs, the Grand Concourse Cafeteria.

In executing the original refurbishment, Arcila-Duque was inspired by the retro feel of this former landmark café and by the time he spent living in New York City. He organized the space into three 'atmospheres': the entrance, the Grand Lounge and the slightly sunken Ultra Lounge at the rear. These areas differ in mood, yet flow into each other, because Arcila-Duque is a man who dislikes restrictions. 'I walk around a space to see how aerodynamic I can make it. I wanted to enhance circulation and create transparency and movement.'

In the lobby, the host desk is positioned in front of a full-height, semi-opaque glass screen (inspired by the Issey Miyake store in SoHo), bearing the MYNT logo. This affords guests blurred views of the Grand Lounge beyond, whilst allowing them to prepare to make their entrance, clearly essential when a venue prides itself on being 'a cool watering hole for the social elite…full of the insanely wealthy mingling with the exaggeratingly beautiful' (as the MYNT website puts it).

The grid pattern of the existing 1950s mint-terrazzo floor set the tone in 2001, guiding A-D to use clean and simple boxy lines. Low sofas, taking a cue from Jean-Michel Frank, were wrapped in dark-grey veneer and, with matching tables, deep club chairs and ottomans, imbued MYNT with the archetypal lounge look.

Two rows of huge, spherical pendant lights, hovering above the furniture, served to define the lounge area within the open-plan space. A keen contemporary art and photography collector, Arcila-Duque incorporated a 12 metre (40 foot) long, wall-mounted lightbox for displaying seasonally rotating images along the wall adjacent to the lounge. Mirroring the lightbox opposite, the bar (of equal length) stretched through the space, constructed from the same grey veneer as the furniture.

above
The ultra-bright VIP lounge.

opposite
Simple, boxy lines and forms characterized the first incarnation of MYNT.

At the rear, a second floor-to-ceiling, semi-opaque glass screen, lit from above, highlighted the DJ while partly concealing the Ultra Lounge, which is dominated by a brightly illuminated perspex bar.

Fast forward two years and A-D has given MYNT a refreshing makeover. 'It got really crowded and everyone danced, but there was no dance floor. So I decided to make it more retro-1970s and psychedelic.' Straight lines have been usurped by 'Jetsons' curves', most dramatically at the entrance, where two organic walls have been sculpted from plaster and then lacquered with car paint. 'I wanted to create a Gehry-influenced, contemporary-cavern feel, and really wanted a metallic finish to emphasize the sculptural effect.'

Inside the lounge, A-D has extended the original terrazzo flooring. 'I continued the terrazzo in glossy, lacquered stripes of the same width up the walls and across the ceiling, to give a tonal feeling of infinity.' Even the air is as fresh as the new palette; the air-conditioning system wafts aromas through the interior, neutralizing the usual nightclub odours.

left
The original 1950s terrazzo floor was the starting point for both design schemes.

The dome lamps and art lightbox were removed, and the latter replaced by a series of back-lit niches, displaying various *objets*, from S&M fetish gear to high-heeled shoes. These are echoed on the opposite wall by bottle-display niches in the back bar.

Orange sofas add contrasting warmth to the green. 'I designed those to give a curved, fit-the-body feeling,' he says. 'The last club was a little too serious. This time I wanted to create happiness.' The DJ remains back-lit (because 'he is the God of the party') by a 'cracked' glass screen, exhibiting giant fissures.

This motif is echoed in the bar façade of the 200-person-capacity Ultra Lounge. Almost entirely green, this space is coated in car paint to achieve luminosity of surface. Arcila-Duque likens it to a 'contemporary version of a neighbourhood basketball court'. Fixed green seating is brightened by durable, orange rubber cushions, and simple, oblong ottomans are multifunctional. Being hollow, they provide storage for belongings and also function as elevated platforms for podium dancing queens.

above
Renderings of the new-look MYNT, with its vibrant-green lacquered interior.

Andy Wahloo / Paris, France

Hassan Hajjij, December 2002

Andy Wahloo is pop-coloured proof that sibling rivalry can produce great things. The conception of this Parisian tapas bar is partly a tale of two brothers – Mourad 'Momo' Mazouz and his younger brother, Hakim. Whilst Momo was wrestling with the creation of multi-million-pound drinking and dining emporium Sketch in London, a building became available just a few doors down from 404, their original Paris restaurant. Hakim swore he could complete the new French bar before Sketch, and on a shoestring budget of 120,000 Euros ($150,000). Hakim 'won', the secret of his success being the Moroccan-born, London-based artist Hassan Hajjij.

Andy Wahloo is a hybrid that reflects Hajjij's dual cultural life and the diversity of his London career, which spans fashion, club promoting, furniture and graphic design. Living in England since his teens, Hajjij began to visit his native country regularly when he became a father. 'I started to want to create work that would celebrate my culture and show it in a positive way,' he says. 'I began by producing canvases. I wasn't interested in making religious or political work, just positive, fun pieces.' This developed into his signature East-meets-West street style, illustrated most succinctly by his picture of iconic, Vuitton-emblazoned *babouches* (Moroccan slippers).

It was the Algerian world-music singer Rachid Taha who first coined the expression Andy Wahloo. 'He fell in love with my work and compared it to Andy Warhol,' explains Hajjij, 'which I took as a compliment. But he said "No. Andy *Wahloo*", which means "I have nothing", and I thought "That's it!"' Hajjij began using the Parisian slang-inspired term as his personal art trademark. The Mazouz brothers commissioned him to create their Paris bar following a London exhibition of the Andy Wahloo work. Considering the limited budget, 'Andy Wahloo' seemed an apt name for the project.

'We describe the look as 70s Pop Art from Morocco,' says Hakim of the quirky interior, curated and assembled by Hajjij. The original street façade remains intact, so the exterior advertizes fashion wholesale – 'Caleçons Pyjamas', 'Fabrique de Chemises' and 'Vêtements de Travail'. This is deliciously subverted by the busy window display of knick-knack-style shelving, packed with grocery products in Arabic packaging.

opposite left
The street façade, with pre-existing fashion-wholesaler signage.

opposite right
Arabic groceries provide colourful window ornamentation.

above
Furniture consists of recycled road signs for tables and paint cans for stools.

above right
Hajjij's East-meets-West artwork, including Louis Vuitton *babouches*, adorns the walls.

Hajjij's eclectic, almost kitsch, interior combines authentic urban detritus from North Africa – reclaimed road signs are recycled as table tops, and Coca-Cola crates function as stools – with delicate handicrafts, such as lanterns and kilim cushions. Floral standard lamps appear to be vintage, but are, in fact, bespoke, using a material from Morocco. 'The fabric was around when I was a small boy and is still used on café parasols and table cloths,' says Hajjij. 'It evokes childhood memories for other Moroccans of my age, too.'

Despite Andy Wahloo's lo-fi, Do-It-Yourself design aesthetic, it's so far proved incredibly popular with the fashion crowd; Vuitton, Armani and Yves Saint Laurent have all held soirées there, and Emmanuelle Béart is a regular. Whether it's the nostalgia, the venue's whimsical nature or simply its anarchic sense of fun, Hajjij's 'I have nothing' is turning out to be quite something.

XL / New York, USA

Desgrippes Gobé Group, April 2001

On the edge of New York's Meatpacking District, and rubbing shoulders with the cool Maritime Hotel, XL is a glowing vision in blue. Desgrippes Gobé Group designer Sam O'Donahue says, 'The render on the façade was also used by the Maritime Hotel, so it looks like the bar is part of the hotel. I love the idea of someone walking into the gayest of gay bars by mistake.'

Formerly a garage, the project took 14 months to complete and cost in excess of $2 million. The brief was relaxed, the only stipulation being that the bar function from early evening until late at night. However, the deep, narrow site lacked windows, which is fine in a club environment, but not ideal for an early-evening cocktail bar. Desgrippes Gobé's solution was to throw light on the matter and install colour-changing lighting systems, a mood-altering technique that has, over the past five years, been used extensively in nocturnal spaces.

'It starts with cool blues and gradually mutates to hedonistic reds until after midnight, when it can strobe and make the entire place feel like a nightclub,' O'Donahue explains. Even the tables change colour; lighting is directed onto the modified-acrylic tops, to create the illusion of internal illumination. In keeping with the atmospheric lighting, images are projected onto the ceiling and upper walls from two banks of projectors, which line the walls at mezzanine level. 'Early-evening blue skies and fluffy clouds decorate the ceiling, but later this changes to crazy graphics or porn, transforming XL from a sophisticated cocktail bar into a nightclub.'

XL comprises a double-height, ground-floor bar, with a mezzanine at the rear, and small, third-floor VIP room above. Like most successful clubs, XL is all about voyeurism and display, enhanced by a little light drama. Desgrippes Gobé were keen to optimize the patron's opportunity for performance through design. Hence the central island bar on the ground floor, perfect for preening, posing and making eyes across the black, polished Corian bar counter.

right
At XL, images and colours projected onto the ceiling dictate the atmosphere.

Even the bespoke bar stools at XL were carefully considered. They are slightly smaller than the smallest mass-manufactured bar stool. 'So you can't slouch, but have to sit with a straight back, otherwise you feel like you're going to fall off,' says O'Donahue. 'Everyone looks like a ballerina with beautiful posture; the stools are sort of self-selecting, so only toned bodies are allowed at the bar.'

Elsewhere, essential elements are designed to provide ample stage for club divas and prima donnas. The open, curved staircase at the rear, which leads up to the mezzanine, is silhouetted against a huge back-lit wall, to encourage theatrical behaviour. 'It's central and in full view of the bar. Early-evening people are coy, but, by the end, people really show off and dance up the stairs.'

The mezzanine bar has a slightly more laid-back ambience, with mirror-clad walls, dressed in diaphanous white drapes, and custom-made chairs, two inches lower than your average lounge chair, to make reclining the only option. A glass balustrade allows patrons on this upper level a prime gallery view of drinkers below. Even the toilets feature spying opportunities; only a long aquarium separates those taking care of business from those washing their hands, and plastic windows between the stalls allow for inter-cubicle flirting.

The voyeurism continues in the raised VIP room, located behind the main stairwell at the rear. Hidden behind a one-way mirrored wall, VIPs can anonymously observe patrons in the top lounge area. They can also survey the overall talent on a series of plasma monitors, recessed into a timber wall. 'There are a set of hidden cameras throughout the bar, so VIPs can control these and even multiply the image of someone they like on every screen.'

O'Donahue admits that 'It may sound like Big Brother, but it's perfect for a cruisy Manhattan gay bar. You know someone's always watching, so you behave, and everyone subconsciously always looks their best.'

left
XL's anonymous façade, with rectilinear apertures, illuminated at night to attract patrons.

below left
Upstairs, halogen lights on stainless-steel rods produce a twinkling galaxy of stars.

opposite
The ground-floor island bar, where small-topped stools force guests to sit most gracefully.

Chapter Two: *Restaurant Bars*

Kong / Paris, France
....
Philippe Starck, May 2003

Perched atop the Kenzo headquarters in Paris, overlooking the Pont Neuf, is Kong. This rainbow-hued cyber-hybrid is the latest creation from the enterprising double act of restaurateur Laurent Taïeb and designer Philippe Starck. Their previous ventures include Paris restaurants Bon and Bon II. For this project, Taïeb asked Starck to immortalize the French capital, whilst respecting the restaurant's association with Kenzo. The restaurateur says, 'All in all, we have come closer to the Kenzo spirit – a Parisian style, with subtle hints towards its native Japan.'

Starck's concept rests on the clash between 'the moderns and the classics'. 'It is the classic of a geisha against the modern *kawai* from Omotesando,' says Starck. 'They meet at the elegant European's at the summit of Kenzo's headquarters. These women finally become one person, timeless and sublime.' This trio of figures, like eternal sirens, form Kong's central motif. Their portraits appear throughout the fifth-floor bar as transfers on the perspex elements that divide seating areas and as three-become-one holograms on the seat backs of the maple rocking chairs.

The focal point of the space is the stainless-steel bar, its poppy-blossom-strewn glass top (inspired by Kenzo's perfume bottle) trailing a blaze of rouge through the room. Starck makes a feature of the spiral stair leading up to the restaurant above by lining it with shelves, littered with an assortment of French and Japanese bric-a-brac – Eiffel Tower souvenirs, sake bottles, Hello Kitty merchandise and so on.

Kong is eclectically Starck; bursts of pop-fluorescent colour and pastel sofas and blinds are juxtaposed with the 'zen pebble rug' and distressed walls. A DJ spins tunes from a punkish, hot-pink Louis XV desk, selecting an 'atomic cocktail' of tunes that receives the majority vote, from categories programmed by DJ Beatrice Ardisson.

above
The bar occupies the lower-top floor of the Kenzo HQ, with the restaurant on the penthouse level above.

above centre
Maple rocking chairs, featuring the ubiquitous holographic faces.

above left
The poppy-blossom bar top's blaze of red.

opposite
A hybrid motif of traditional Geisha, modern-day, trendy Japanese woman and stylish European woman is repeated, in the form of holographic portraits, throughout.

Himmelreich / Mülheim, Germany

Jordan Mozer & Associates, January 2003

In a world full of superbrands, long-established companies are revitalizing themselves, usually through design, to keep up with the twenty-first century's style-savvy consumer. Europe's largest retailer, Karstadt, is one such company. Around 100 years old and with 150 department stores across the continent, it was desperately in need of reinvention. Chicago-based designer Jordan Mozer, who has been creating projects in Germany for over a decade, stepped in to refurbish an existing mammoth 40,000 square metre (430,000 square foot) Karstadt store in Mülheim, a densely inhabited suburb of Düsseldorf.

In creating the Karstadt Lifestyle Department Store, Mozer applied lessons learnt whilst working on entertainment projects in the US. 'Las Vegas is the place where these hybrid ideas really blossomed. To attract guests to their casinos, our astute clients realized that the American's favourite form of entertainment is shopping,' he says, 'especially when catalyzed with complementary entertainment and restaurant service concepts.'

Armed with a budget of $50 per 0.1 square metre (1 square foot), they modernized the megastore (originally built in the 1970s), radically redesigning circulation and addressing the 'lack of punctuation' by organizing the diverse products into 'streets' of individual stores, to give the overall space cohesion. They also recognized that no hip new department store is complete without a cool café-bar and cocktail lounge: thus we have Himmelreich, which means 'kingdom of heaven'.

Himmelreich's retro aesthetic of curvy geometric shapes, in a white and taupe palette, is specific to the second floor, also home to women's fashion. The café and cocktail bar are positioned opposite the main entrance, at the far end of the floor, to lure customers through the space.

'The design borrows from a mid-twentieth-century vision of the future to imagine the future of Karstadt in the 21st century. We looked at what was happening in luxury brands, such as Gucci, Vuitton and Prada and were inspired by the 1960s modern design. We warmed it all up though,' explains Mozer.

The 600 square metre (6,450 square foot) bar and café accommodates 165 people, and has its own separate street entrance, so that it can operate independently from, and later than, the store. There are various different areas, including a long bar and a raised cocktail lounge, with low chairs. Himmelreich's geometric motifs, present in the lanterns, plaster ceiling, floor and screens, can be found throughout the second floor. The patterned floor is composed of vinyl tiles. These forms are repeated in the screens and the lanterns, where they are constructed from laser-cut, heat-formed milk-coloured acrylic.

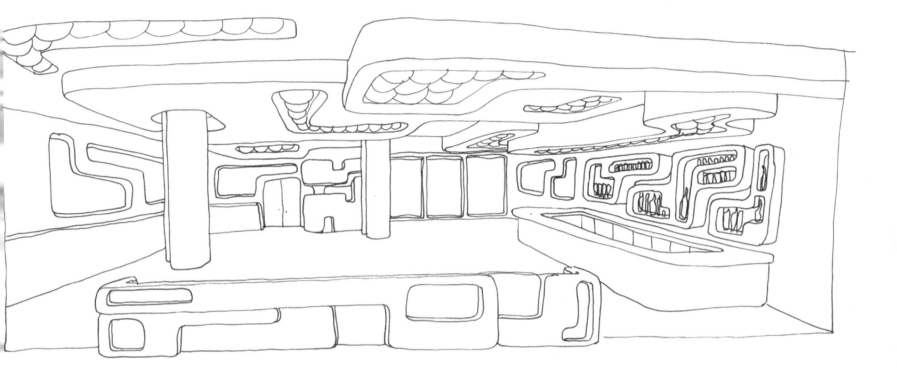

above
An early sketch reveals how the geometric motif is repeated in the back-bar shelving.

left
A view of Himmelreich from the mall, framed by curvy, geometric-shaped screens.

opposite
Raised cocktail-lounge area, with its low-slung chairs.

Crystal / Beirut, Lebanon

Gatserelia Design International, June 2003

Beirut nightlife is firmly back on the party map, with the many bars and clubs on flashy, nocturnal strip Monot Street proving to be an alluring magnet for Mediterranean locals and cosmopolitan jetsetters from Syria, Jordan, Egypt and Turkey. Crystal is a popular venue, designed by native Gatserelia Design International to 'attract the night owls of the area'. 'We decided, with the clients, to come up with a cool space, almost verging on the flashy, a space reminiscent of the 1950s to 1970s clubs dedicated to the Cuban drug lords operating in Miami, à la *Scarface*,' explains Gregory Gatserelia.

Crystal has certainly got bling. The plain street façade belies the glitzy interior, which consists of a 350 square metre (3,800 square foot) volume, with two mezzanines and with mirrored walls, providing plenty of sight lines. As Gatserelia says, 'we made it one spacious room to ensure success, because, by enhancing the opportunity to "see and be seen", you elevate the club atmosphere to a more intense level.' Aside from the sheer scale of the venue, it is the combination of retro lighting, metallic finishes and ornate plasterwork that imbues Crystal with glamour.

At the centre of the space, a gleaming bespoke chandelier emits a warm glow, which transforms the stainless-steel ceiling dome into a halo of gold. And then there's the main bar. The simple counter, topped with glossy ceramic tiles, tough enough to withstand dancing, is illuminated by the mirrored back bar, which features bold plasterwork, framing three reproductions of the iconic 'Pistillino' lamp (Studio Tetrach, 1969). These elements appear elsewhere – the plasterwork-patterned mirror is repeated on the mezzanine, and pendant lights throughout are of a similar 1960s-style chrome design.

The wrought-iron balcony rails, surrounding the mezzanines, echo the geometric forms of the retro light pieces. They are painted white, as is the flamboyant ironwork decorating one wall, 'to give a lace look'. Gatserelia describes this floral-patterned environment as 'very David Hicks'. Furniture throughout was custom-designed to suggest the 1940s and 1950s. 'Tables, stools, chairs and sofas are the dancing spots, so they look refined, but are well-structured and strongly built. Fabrics come from a variety of sources and are constantly renewed because they endure such a pounding.'

plan, opposite top
Two mezzanines create different levels, adding to the 'see and be seen' atmosphere.

opposite
The stainless-steel ceiling dome is lent a golden hue by Gatserelia's bespoke chandelier.

below
Tentacled 1960s 'Pistillino' lamps are the star attraction of the back bar.

Crystal has inspired a term to describe Beirut's new hedonism: 'the Crystal Effect' (*Crystaliyeie* in Arabic), which *Vanity Fair* magazine chose to translate as 'champagne and show'. Purchasing colossal bottles of champagne at Crystal is a show-stopping event; the music stops, the lights go down and the buyer is spotlit, as he (as it is mostly) receives the order. Buyers of magnums are invited to engrave their name on the board by the door, leaving their mark behind – surely the ultimate in blinging decoration.

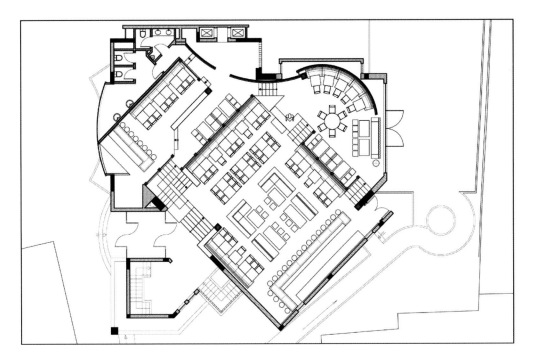

Nectar / Las Vegas, USA

Jordan Mozer & Associates, September 2001

Las Vegas, city of neon and artifice, lends itself to fantastical design. Enter Chicago-based designer Jordan Mozer, a man whose organic, sculptural forms imbue interiors with a playful vitality. Asked to refurbish a restaurant and bar in the Bellagio Hotel and Casino Resort, Mozer responded by creating Nectar.

The distinctive restaurant space, with its bone-like columns, was inspired by the use of trees in the indigenous, primitive architecture of the American Southwest, with additional references to Gaudí's architecture and Brancusi's sculpture. The column device has been extended into the futuristic 33-seat bar, but here the surroundings are distinctly cooler than the warm, rustic restaurant interior.

'Las Vegas is really hot, and it's a dry heat,' says Mozer, 'so in the bar I wanted to emulate melted ice and a cooling atmosphere.' The small bar space is suggestive of an ultra-bright space capsule. Fluid, 'melting' forms and smooth, polished surfaces create a 'liquid-cool' aesthetic. The epoxy-based terrazzo floor, inlaid with blue-glass chunks, curves up to form the bar itself and wraps around the base of a large, central column. This trunk rises up to form a mushroom-like, illuminated coffer over the space. Lighting is relatively diffuse, reflecting off the white surfaces to give a lunar-like glow.

Shiny, white stools, constructed from Kevlar-reinforced resin, complete the icy, futuristic look. 'This is a tough, non-combustible material, also used to make bullet-proof police vests; so they're bullet-proof bar stools,' jokes Mozer. Whereas the restaurant is designed for relaxed dining, the bar is a far more stimulating space and acoustically louder. It forms the transition point between the casino and the exclusive designer retail corridor, which houses designer brands like Gucci, Prada and Chanel. To ensure that this stylish haven remains enticingly on view to passing high rollers and big spenders, Mozer enclosed the bar with a simple set of custom-designed railings, in cast magnesium aluminium.

plan
The small bar affords guests
a cool alternative to the
adjoining Nectar restaurant.
1. entry, 2. bar, 3. dining,
4. kitchen

left
Custom-made, shiny white
bar stools are made from a
tough, bullet-proof material.

opposite
The mushroom column
features recessed lighting
to create a canopy of light
over guests.

Megu / New York, USA

Glamorous, March 2004

Osaka-born designer Yasumichi Morita and his team have created numerous restaurants and bars throughout their native Japan, and also in Hong Kong. More recently, they have expanded overseas, and Megu is their stunning New York debut.

Presented with a capacious 14,000 square metre (150,000 square foot) site in a downtown TriBeCa location, Morita was asked to create an interior that 'represents the "true Japan" that fascinates New Yorkers.' He decided to offer the discerning, cosmopolitan locals a choice. 'Megu is not only a place for eating, but also for entertainment,' says Morita. 'I wanted them to create several different scenes, so that the guests could choose their table depending on their mood or occasion.'

A void was created, through excavation, below ground level in order to accommodate the two-tiered venue. The main, double-height dining room, adjoining Sushi & Charcoal Bar and the Royal Miyabi Room are all situated on the basement level. The Kimono Bar and the Imperial Lounge are located on the ground floor, close to the entrance and reception. 'I believe that the dining room should be cosy, with a warm atmosphere, and that the bar and lounge should have a different atmosphere,' explains Morita. 'Bars should feel exciting, as this is where people want to socialize and mingle.'

right
A 'Rising Sun' screen, composed of sake bottles and rice bowls, signals Megu's presence at street level.

opposite
The corridor leading to the Kimono Bar is flanked by the same sake bottle and rice bowl screens, backlit and encased behind glass.

Japanese crafts and artefacts are intelligently integrated throughout Megu to produce an eastern aura. Passers-by are alerted to the venue's presence by a decorative screen, bearing the 'Rising Sun' flag, which is clearly visible through the lofty warehouse windows of the façade. The screen is composed of sake bottles and rice bowls, stacked in towers, glued and held together by a rod and bolt. This kind of alchemy, transforming authentic Japanese elements into a contemporary design, continues inside.

Entering guests pass through a low-lit, sombre passageway and reception area, lined in grey ceramic tiles and featuring display cabinets. The corridor approach to the Kimono Bar houses Megu's iconic porcelain towers, back-lit from below and set behind glass. In contrast to the cool, muted tones of the reception, the Kimono Bar itself is a vibrant, deep-scarlet shrine to the exquisite prints of this traditional Japanese form of dress.

The central, 'catwalk' black-granite bar is crowned by a patchwork runner, fabricated from multi-coloured panels of antique obi, the sash fastened at the back of the kimono in a bow. This decorative panel is fixed to the ceiling in the aisle created by the bar's overhead cabinets. These units provide glass storage and also accommodate the spotlights that illuminate the patchwork runner above.

Enriching the space further are horizontal bars of kimono fabric, lining two walls. The remaining walls are painted gloss red. The rich, womb-like interior is reinforced by the floor, with its various shades of stained mahogany, and by the oil-stained cherrywood tables. Patrons are seated either side of the central bar on cream leather-upholstered booths and bespoke chairs.

Whereas as the Kimono Bar is an exotic, enclosed drinking den, the Imperial Lounge is more about surveying the restaurant scene below. Positioned at the head of the rectilinear, sunken, main dining room and contained behind floor-to-ceiling glazing, this bar affords regal views.

above
The glass-storage unit above the bar also houses spotlights that illuminate the patchwork strip.

right
In the Kimono Bar, a patchwork runner of antique obi, fixed to the ceiling, runs the length of the island bar.

Furniture is organized to optimize the voyeuristic experience, with a series of throne-like, padded, cream-leather booths lining the rear wall. Simple, parallel booths are positioned next to the glazing, allowing all occupants a bird's-eye view.

Mahogany flooring and cherrywood tables elevate the space and add a natural, Japanese flavour. As ever with a Glamorous project, Morita's lighting is one of the star attractions. Each booth is lit by a diagonal constellation of delicate, custom-designed lanterns. 'These are modelled on Japanese lanterns for Buddhist altars, made of bronze and plated with fine gold.' At Megu, it seems that 'true Japan' really is in the detail.

above left
View of the Imperial Lounge from the dining room below.

above
The Imperial Lounge is furnished with high-backed booths, upholstered in padded cream leather.

above
Japanese details continue in
the women's toilets.

left
View from the Imperial
Lounge of the dining room
below, complete with
Buddhist temple bell.

The Loft / Sydney, Australia

Dale Jones-Evans Architects, June 2003

Sydney is not a city dense with richly decorated bar interiors. It is, in essence, all about the great outdoors. In a culture where barbecues are the national cuisine, a sophisticated urban bar and restaurant scene, comparable with London or New York, has been a relatively new development. Indeed, until the early 1990s, many venues were incredibly simple, with unadorned, café-like interiors that did not detract from the views of blue skies, harbours and beaches outside their windows.

In this context, the intricately patterned interior of The Loft, by Dale Jones-Evans Architects, is quite extraordinary. Internationally celebrated architect Jones-Evans established his practice in 1984. Known best for its pioneering residential works, one of its more recent commercial projects was the 2001 refurbishment of the Sydney Opera House's Bennelong restaurant, in which it incorporated Aboriginal painted lamps and memorial totem poles, as a symbolic act of reclamation of the ground upon which the opera house stands.

The Loft is linked to Bungalow 8, and together they occupy the ground and first floors of a new building that is part of the Philip Cox-designed King Street Wharf waterfront development. Dale Jones-Evans was asked to design two bar-restaurant venues that were linked, but had separate identities. The Loft was conceived as 'an immersive painting, composed of different ambient lighting conditions'. To connect the two venues, Dale Jones-Evans constructed a dramatic, dark-stained plywood lightbox, animated by striated patternation, around which wraps the internal circulation stair. 'The link grows out of Bungalow 8's texture (which features a bamboo ceiling and paper lanterns) and becomes part of the intense patternation of The Loft while standing independently as an *objet d'art*,' writes Jones-Evans.

By day, the decadent, 500-capacity venue operates as a tapas bar, transforming later into a cocktail lounge bar. Inside, decorative, laser-cut Pacific Cedar Marine plywood screens, ambient lighting and the toffee and caramel hues of timber and leather furnishings combine to exude a honeyed warmth. 'Artifice and abstraction, femininity and patternation compress to generate an immersive, seductive and sumptuous environment of texture and light,' explains Jones-Evans. The floral-patterned back wall extends up over the ceiling, wrapping up the room in fine foliage. Cosy seating areas are partly concealed by bolder, lacquered screens, bearing a geometric design suggestive of honeycomb.

above
Pacific Cedar Marine plywood screens add pattern and divide the interior.

opposite
A striated light box animates the stairwell connecting Bungalow 8 with The Loft.

overleaf
The New Guinea Blackbean bar, crowned by tangerine chandeliers of Spanish beads.

Chapter 2: Restaurant Bars

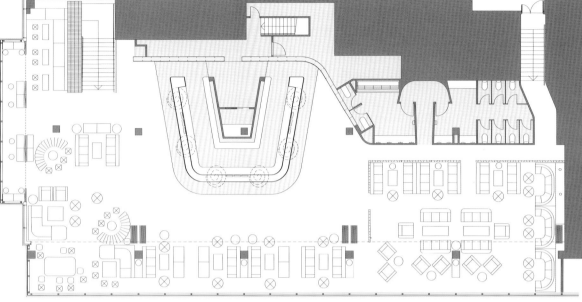

Lighting has been designed in conjunction with the laser-cut screens to create an intriguing interplay of light and shadow in an intimate atmosphere. The back bar is backlit, the floral ceiling screens are bathed in pools of light and, elsewhere, light is refracted through objects, such as the saffron chandeliers, which are fashioned from strands of Spanish beads. These six tangerine gems hang directly above the horseshoe-shaped bar, echoing its form and emphasizing the sculpted solidity of the New Guinea Blackbean bar counter and stainless-steel top.

Deep club chairs and button-studded, leather booth banquettes were custom-designed with comfort in mind, 'to be over-scaled, soft, padded and cigar-like'. The walls are the art, but there is also a piece by artist Dani Marti – a wall relief, comprising red ropes that are interwoven to form a strong pattern of diagonals, in keeping with the venue's richly patterned aesthetic.

The Loft also has a terrace, which Jones-Evans describes as a 'powerful "in-out" space, with an address to the public domain (the wharf) and the externalities of water (harbour), shipping, land edge and the intensity of Australian light'. So, although it may appear to be out of the ordinary, the venue is certainly rooted on terra firma.

plan
Up to 500 people can be accommodated in the 506 square metre (5,450 square foot) venue, with the U-shaped bar at the centre.

left
The low-lit lounge is enclosed by laser-cut plywood screens.

left
One of the seating booths, inspired by the caves of Okinawa.

right
Bottles are displayed in red-lit nooks, and the bar is topped by a red-tiled roof.

Ashibina / Tokyo, Japan

Zokei Syudan Design, October 2001

Beware the giant Ryukyu 'lion-dog' scaling the façade of the Ashibina restaurant-bar in Tokyo's Shinbashi district. This fierce-looking creature, known as 'Shi-sa', hails from Japan's most southerly point, the tropical islands of Okinawa. It is the custom for islanders to display these protective deities on the distinctive, red-tiled roofs of their homes. Ashibina is designed by Okinawa-born architect and designer Yusaku Kaneshiro, and both the food (Korean and Okinawan grill) and design concept are inspired by this once-independent region of Japan.

Since establishing his Tokyo-based studio Zokei Syudan Design in 2000, Kaneshiro's four-strong team have been incredibly prolific, creating over 500 restaurants and bars in Japan. Kaneshiro employs a homegrown, organic aesthetic, using natural materials, such as tree branches, pebbles, *washi* paper, and bamboo, to concoct other-worldly interiors akin to scenes from a futuristic movie. Most of his projects include intriguing pockets of space and beguilingly diffuse lighting. His design objective is 'to make something that doesn't exist, something completely new that no one has seen before, using natural materials'.

Although Ashibina is located on the fourth floor of a building, Kaneshiro has created an interior evocative of a magical, subterranean forest and of grottos, lit by deep-red lanterns. Twisted and tangled branches arch up to form a jungle canopy, with ceiling spotlights partly concealed to create the illusion of 'sunlight flickering through the trees'. Seating booths are a reference to the famous caves of Okinawa. In the Second World War, the caves became natural air-raid shelters for civilians and Japanese soldiers.

Other elements of Kaneshiro's playful homage to his native land include a crazy-paved floor, resembling the ancient, stone streets of Okinawa, and the bar, which is set below a traditional, red-tiled roof, an example (like the Shi-sa) of Chinese influence in this region. Red is the traditional colour of Okinawa, and Kaneshiro has used it to imbue certain parts of Ashibina's earthy interior with a fiery hue. The glowing, red bottle-display nooks of the back bar echo the red-lit caverns and the mouths of the gargoyle-like Shi-sas – all crimson beacons, guiding patrons through the space.

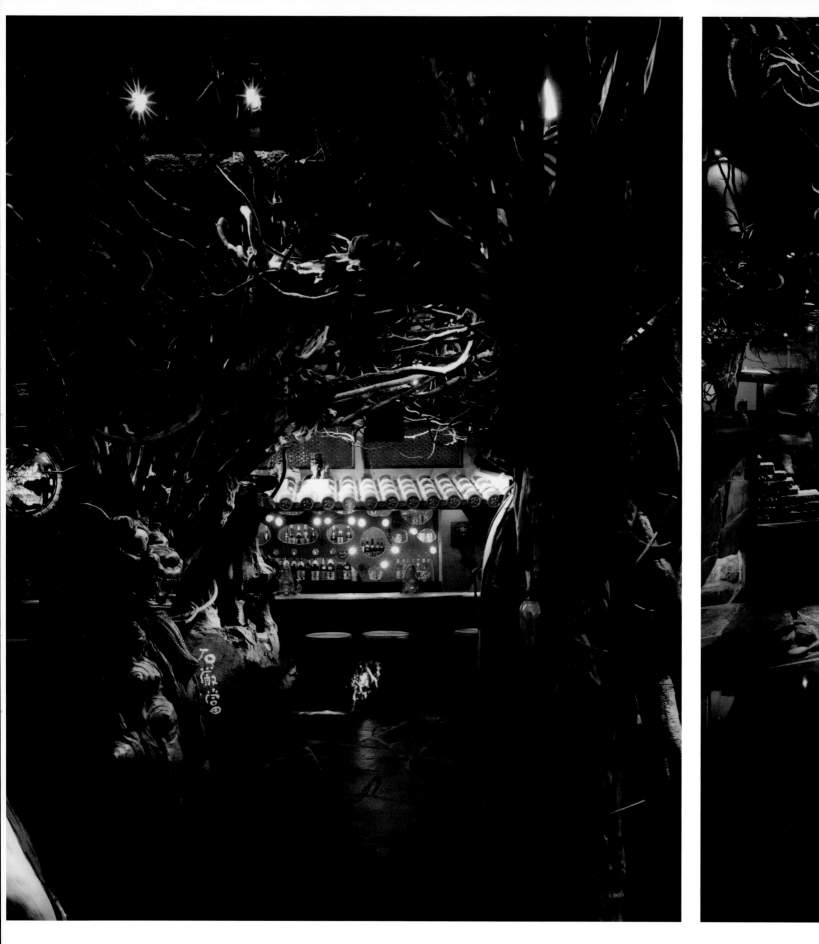

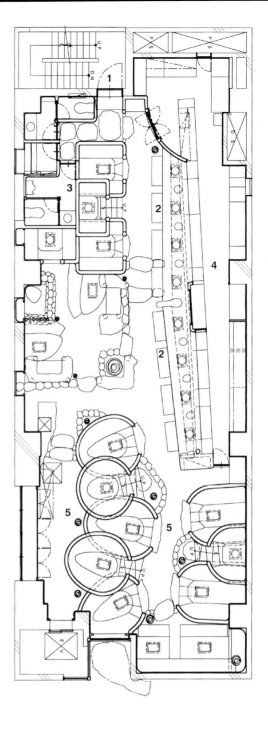

plan
Aside from the bar, seating is
organized in booths designed
to resemble caves.
1, entrance, 2. bar, 3. toilets,
4. kitchen, 5. 'cave' booths

left
Fierce, gargoyle-like 'Shi-sa'
guard Ashibina.

opposite
A jungle of twigs and
branches conceals spotlights,
which flicker, like sunlight,
through the growth.

Zenzibar Lounge / Shanghai, China

AFSO, October 2003

Shanghai is recapturing its decadent youth. This cosmopolitan city, once known as the 'Paris of the Orient', may have been dulled by years of Communism, but now it's back in glorious Technicolor. The old French Quarter, known as Xin Tian Di (meaning 'a new heaven and earth'), has undergone substantial redevelopment and now harbours much of the city's new nightlife. Many of these destination venues occupy the renovated interiors of the area's nineteenth-century mansions, which are known as *Shikumen* ('stone gate'), after their elaborate, stone-framed entrances.

London-based architects AFSO (André Fu and Stéphane Orsolini) created Zenzibar in one such house. The 380 square metre (4,090 square foot) restaurant and bar are located on the ground floor of the period property and form 'stage two' of a scheme that began with the construction of the Zen Chinese restaurant on the first floor. Principal architect André Fu says, 'Zenzibar is designed to provoke a sense of bubbly optimism. It's about Courrèges-meets-Vivien-Tam, or space-age-mod-meets-China.' Aiming to promote 'hope, joy, freedom and innocence', AFSO have combined an array of textures, patterns and forms to produce this design-rich venue.

Patrons entering the 40-cover bar encounter a 'sheer dreamscape of fluidity', boldly expressed by the giant cocoon structure, clad in natural-oak slats, which masquerades as a backdrop to the lounge, but which is also an enclosure for the four private dining salons. The undulating curves of this highly sculptural form create an intimate seating area in the lounge, including a cosy booth, crowned by a trumpet chandelier that complements the small, circular space. Echoing these organic contours is a low, bone-shaped communal table, made of white Corian. Positioned in the centre of the lounge area, it effectively aids circulation, as its curvy, elongated shape guides guests into the heart of the space and towards the stairway access to the Zen Chinese restaurant upstairs.

left
Seats upholstered in French taffeta, bearing a monochrome chintz, reinforce the pattern-rich decadence.

opposite
The circular seating booth, crowned by a trumpet-shaped pendant light.

plan
1. entrance, 2. communal table, 3. private dining salon, 4. kitchen

above
Cherry-blossom-pink light radiates from the decorative screen opposite the horizontally slatted dining cocoon.

opposite
A low, bone-shaped white table provides the focus for communal seating.

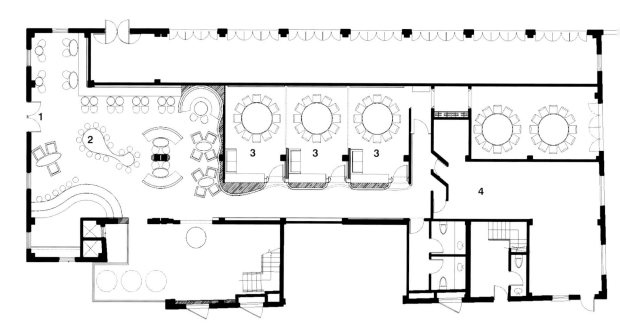

Chapter 2: Restaurant Bars

In Zenzibar, few surfaces are left undecorated; a complex grid of off-white, hexagonal tiles adorns the ceiling, and a low banquette borders walls, covered in bespoke floral, and again hexagonal, tiles. Chairs are upholstered in a flamboyant, monochrome chintz of French taffeta, embossed with velvet, which continues the floral theme.

Lighting adds warmth and sets Zenzibar aglow. The support column, clad in strips of bronze mirror, is topped by a 4 metre (13 foot) diameter half sphere, which incorporates recessed lighting, creating a halo effect. Fu also introduced an extensive back-lit element to the 18 metre (60 foot) long corridor that leads to the private dining salons – a 4 metre (13 foot) high, vertical, criss-crossing frame, constructed from stained-black oak and opaque glass. Radiating shades of peach and cherry-blossom pink, the diagonal pattern, juxtaposed with the horizontal slats of the cocoon, serves to 'heighten the aspect of scale and volume in a linear mode'. The mirrored ceiling adds depth and was introduced to 'enhance this visual play of perspective'.

Zenzibar displays an eclectic mix of influences, much like its host city, Shanghai. As AFSO say, 'Be it a touch of kitsch European sci-fi fantasy or oriental authenticity, the lounge could be described as a theatre of juxtaposing cultural metaphors.'

TMSK / Shanghai, China

Loretta Yang Hui-shan and Chang Yi, December 2004

TMSK restaurant, located in the thriving Xintiandi Plaza, embodies the exuberant spirit of Shanghai's decadent past and its glamorous twenty-first-century renaissance. The interior glows with the extravagant Chinese art of *liuli*, an exquisite, coloured crystal, the origins of which date back centuries. The project is the culmination of years of glass craftsmanship by highly acclaimed artisan Loretta Yang Hui-shan and her husband Chang Yi, as suggested by the name of the venue – Tao Ming Si Kao – which translates as 'transparent thought'.

Yang Hui-shan retired from a successful acting career in 1986 to focus on a lifelong interest in *liuli* art. Since then, she has exhibited in the USA, France and in her native Taiwan, and has developed the popular Liuli Gong Fang brand, with boutiques across Asia selling her crystal jewellery and other *objets*. These pieces are crafted using the pâte-de-verre technique, a mould-based system that was more recently used by Art Nouveau artists, but also echoes the bronze-making methods of the Shang and Zhou periods of China. It is possible that the Chinese used this production technique as long as 2,000 years ago.

TMSK features a restaurant, Little Stage, for theatrical performances, and a bar. It is a veritable *liuli* gallery: 'everything within sight and touch is made of, or partly of, *liuli*, including the bar, the orchid pond, the screens, the walls, the vaulted ceiling, the floors, the windows, the tables and the chairs, the lamps and lanterns, the tableware and so on.'

Lighting throughout the interior is low and diffuse to allow the *liuli* to shine. 'Sunlight is filtered out, and much is done to enrich and heighten the artistic effect of almost every invisible detail,' explains Yang Hui-shan. The bar is a crystal showcase, bright and vibrant against the black Chinese-tiled floor and black ceiling. Its blue and green glass-tiled façade appears rainbow-hued, due to the reflection of the bar stools. These are fabricated from glass discs, resting on traditional-style silk lanterns, internally lit to glow cerise. Heightening the dramatic effect is the shimmering, golden back bar.

Seating booths housing lip-shaped chairs, upholstered in silk brocade, are separated from the main bar area by clear-glass walls, inset with a square metre (11 square feet) of coloured-glass chips, providing privacy. Completing the artistic display is the Orchid Pond, a platform of black tiles inlaid with illuminated, green-glass tiles that sprout delicate glass flowers.

left
The multi-coloured *liuli* is reflected in the golden foil, making TMSK gleam in rainbow shades.

Villa Zévaco / Casablanca, Morocco

Andy Martin Associates, February 2004

Since establishing his studio in 1996, Antipodean architect Andy Martin has carved out for himself a distinctive niche in the realm of restaurant and bar design in his adopted city of London. His style has been aptly described by a fellow architect as 'imaginative, timeless and cool'. Notable projects include Mash and Isola, which reveal a comprehensive, holistic approach, with AMA taking care to design every detail, while not forgetting the bigger picture. Villa Zévaco is no exception.

Being asked to transform a listed, three-bedroom villa in the affluent Anfa district of Casablanca into a gastronomic emporium, including a boulangerie, pâtisserie, salon de thé, restaurant, bar and function space, was challenge enough. Yet this was no ordinary villa. Originally called Villa Suisse (while nicknamed 'The Butterfly') and built in 1947, the stunning white house was designed by celebrated architect Jean-François Zévaco.

Throughout the extensive renovation, AMA endeavoured to respect Zévaco's legacy, bringing the villa into the twenty-first century without losing its architectural integrity. 'We re-landscaped the entire grounds,' explains Martin. 'Everything links up on the building layout plan on a radius. We took that further and assumed what he would have done.'

Main services and kitchens were placed in the newly extended basement of the house, and two approximately 100 square metre (1,080 square foot) wings were added either side of the main body to accommodate the pâtisserie on one side and the Library cocktail bar on the other. For the latter, AMA took their inspiration from Zévaco's work and from a mid-twentieth-century aesthetic, whilst lending the space their own particular signature style. 'When you're doing something like this, you have to pick classic references for it to work,' says Martin. Natural materials of slate, timber and leather have been combined with fluid contours, elementary colours and monochrome. 'There is nothing superfluous. Decorative elements are only used as part of the fabric of the architecture,' such as the sliding glass entrance doors and the terrazzo floor.

The abstract metal design of the entrance is loosely based on Zévaco. 'We carried a theme of linear lines throughout the villa. This was our own graphic interpretation of his design,' explains Martin. Ditto the fun, pebble-patterned floor. 'In the 1950s, they designed floors with marble off-cuts laid into terrazzo. It was common in Morocco, France and Italy. So we used nero absoluto marble to accentuate the 1950s style. We thought we'd have fun, give it a dynamic shape and put our mark on it.'

All furniture is custom-made, in a light palette of white with pale-blue-suede accents, as befitting the hot climate. High-backed chairs were designed as 'homages to Gio Ponti', and timber coffee tables feature 1950s-style angled legs with brass details. 'As it's the library, these were designed as timber boxes, with bright interiors for displaying books,' says Martin. Vintage standard lamps were purchased in London, and timber blinds at the windows add warmth. Period authenticity is enhanced by exposed slate walls, reclaimed by AMA from demolished parts of the original villa, which was constructed from this natural material native to the coast of Casablanca.

747 Bar / Syracuse, Sicily

L.A. Design, September 2003

The slender, modern steel-and-glass façade of 747 Bar contrasts sharply with the noble, eighteenth-century streets of Syracuse, and that's the whole point. Italian designer Leonardo Annecca was asked to import 'the vibrancy of Miami Beach' to the traditional, baroque Sicilian town by Dambaloo, a group of local developers. Faced with the challenge of refurbishing a deep, narrow 128 square metre (1,380 square foot) space, lacking in natural light, Annecca decided that a 'fresh, airline-cabin interior' was the answer.

The Milan-born designer was inspired by his own peripatetic, jet-set lifestyle. Annecca spends much of his time in Boeing 747s, flying between his New York office and his Paris studio. 'The concept comes from L.A.'s flight-attendant soul!,' he says. 'This is an attitude towards life, where planes still represent the image of freedom and the dream of flying amongst stars and clouds.'

The venue is located only minutes from the Duomo, in a protected architectural zone, making the biggest challenge for L.A. to convince the authorities that such a radical departure from the traditional, vernacular architecture of the area was a good idea. However, Annecca won them over, and 747 Bar was one of the first contemporary projects in Syracuse to receive a building permit. It was a long time in the making, though; the construction period was delayed twice by the discovery of archaeological ruins on the site and also affected somewhat by 'the Sicilian manual workers' rhythm'.

The clear-glass doors, with a polished stainless-steel frame, reveal the glowing Cockpit Bar and the stainless-steel, arched opening (concealing existing columns and air-conditioning) that signals the threshold of the restaurant lounge beyond. Annecca's choice of materials, retro-futuro curves and ambient, pastel lighting conjure up a sense of optimism, the anachronistic notion of being airborne and in pleasurable limbo, unlike the anxiety we associate with air travel today.

right
Clear-glass doors, framed by
polished stainless steel,
reveal the Cockpit Bar to
passers-by.

The focal point of the Cockpit Bar is its circular bar, constructed from translucent perspex panels, which contain fluorescent tubes, wrapped in differently coloured gelatine films. In keeping with the industrial, airline-cabin theme, the bar is finished with a stainless-steel base and counter top, which houses recessed neon lighting. The perspex and fluorescent-tubing effect is repeated in the dramatic floor-to-ceiling dividing screen and backdrop to the bar. Bartenders can control the mood by altering the intensity of the different light hues. The rest of the bar interior enhances these lighting effects. The floor of poured, white-rubber resin and the layer of white drapes concealing the Trevira walls, reflect the changing light colours.

In the glossy, white restaurant lounge, furnished with bespoke, white furniture, warmth is created by the intense orange glow emanating from recessed, horizontal channels, which house fluorescent tubes, again set behind perspex, at mid-height and floor level, beneath the banquettes. Above diners' heads, a suspended, tubular unit contains the air-conditioning, whilst also operating as an acoustic absorber, so nothing detracts from the streamline aesthetic.

747's second bar, at the rear of the restaurant, mirrors the first in form and materials, except that the expansive, illuminated screen is replaced by a modest, glowing chartreuse wall, featuring a glowing bottle display. Aviation is in the detail, with the plastic panels fixed with hexagonal screws, as typically seen in aircraft.

Later in the evening, the restaurant morphs into a club and dancers perform on a small stage at the front of the restaurant, creating intriguing silhouettes against the dividing screen for drinkers in the Cockpit Bar. In-flight entertainment extends beyond the visual, aural, tactile and gastronomic on this 747 – Annecca's intention that his creation should stimulate all the senses is completed by the scent of Sicilian clementines, which is vaporized into the space by the air-conditioning system. If only all airline cabins smelt so sweet.

top
Changing lighting elements, controlled by the bartenders, determine the mood of the bar.

above
The restaurant behind the bar morphs into a club later in the evening.

Hajime / Tokyo, Japan

Glamorous, February 2002

Master of illusion Yasumichi Morita and his Glamorous team have performed an optical trick once again at this miniscule bar in Tokyo's exclusive, designer shopping district of Ginza. Using limited lighting, Morita has created phantom depth in a space that measures less than 40 square metres (430 square feet). Indeed, the front-of-house bar area occupies only half of the total space, rendering any design scheme a challenge.

'Although there are limits to what we can design for such a small space,' says Morita, 'I thought that I could turn this disadvantage into an advantage.' In such a restricted interior, Morita decided that light should be the only decoration. A glowing framework of lighting was constructed from rows of mini Krypton lamps, dimmed to 30 per cent of their brightness and enclosed in polycarbonate board and graphic sheet, similar to the texture of Japanese parchment.

Some surfaces and furniture are blackened to fade into obscurity, while others are polished to reflect the clean lines of the lighting. The ceiling is painted with black, acrylic emulsion, the floor lined with black, vinyl tiles, while seating is upholstered in black vinyl and the walls are either covered in textured wallpaper or mirrored to maximize the sense of space. The focal point of the venue is the illuminated eight-seater bar, which is topped by stained Assamela timber and clear polyurethane to produce a polished surface. Additional seating is provided by a table for six.

Morita's structured lighting system not only emphasizes important elements of the interior, but also signals the presence of the bar to those outside at street level. The channel of light starts at the exterior signage and runs along a wall, guiding patrons down the alley towards the bar entrance, where it terminates. Inside, the path of light moves vertically from the floor of the bar up the wall, illuminating the bar area.

right
Inside, the interior is a strong contrast of light and shadow.

opposite left
The eight-seater bar, with its illuminated framework, is the centrepiece.

opposite right
Street signage, which lights the way to the entrance.

Supperclubcruise / Amsterdam, Netherlands

Concrete, October 2003

Dutch design firm Concrete have created a nocturnal dreamboat for Supperclub lovers. Since the original Supperclub opened in Amsterdam in 1999, the ethereal reclining-dining club concept has proved immensely popular, spawning a sequel in Rome and numerous imitators around the world. Supperclubcruise is the third IQ Creative venture (more are planned in San Francisco and London), and, like its predecessors, it features the sexy, dark Le Bar Noir, offering cocktails and disco action, and the all-white Salle Neige, which houses a colossal chrome, steel-framed bed that can accommodate up to 75 diners.

The main challenge for Concrete was having to design a venue without a fixed abode. 'Supperclubcruise doesn't have a final location, so it had to be strong within itself,' explains designer Rob Wagemans. 'Sometimes it may be in a beautiful harbour, sometimes ugly. It could be on a large river, or a small one. So it had to be designed as an absolute entity in itself.' The windows in the bar have grey-tinted glass, 'so you can look outside, but the world is a little bit darker, and downstairs, in Salle Neige, you can't look outside at all, so you are completely lost and escape external reality.'

A further test for the design team was sourcing materials that would adhere to the stringent fire and safety regulations, something Concrete took in their stride, whilst managing to maintain Supperclub's strong visual identity. There are colour-coded resin floors throughout, in keeping with the dominant scheme of each area; red in the entrance and toilets, black in Le Bar Noir and white in Salle Neige. Supperclub's trademark unisex toilets, also a 'destination' for socializing, are given a sense of luxury by red carpeting, which wraps up to cover the walls, and by a skirting of polished stainless steel.

In Le Bar Noir, a shiny, high-gloss black 'stretch ceiling' has a dark mirroring effect, maximizing the sense of space in a predominantly black interior. Interaction between guests is encouraged by the sculptural, black mock-croc leather banquette, which snakes through the space, creating booths and throwing strangers together. Chrome pedestal tables, with black tops, complete the look.

Below deck, Salle Neige's mellow atmosphere is enhanced by digitally programmed lighting, which drenches the interior in gradually changing rainbow hues. The effect is created by lighting tubes, installed behind the polycarbonate wall panelling, setting the entire space aglow. The ceiling was stripped back to reveal the existing basic construction and painted white. 'It is high enough so that guests can dance on the beds without knocking their heads,' says Wagemans.

Supperclubcruise will travel to any European port for corporate/group bookings. Otherwise, it harbours guests in Amsterdam. 'The whole premise of the Supperclub is to take guests away from society, to forget everything just for one night,' explains Wagemans. 'The great thing about Supperclubcruise is that the experience intensifies, becoming even more physical, because you leave the mainland and go floating down the river.' Forget plain sailing – let's cruise!

above
Below deck, Salle Neige accommodates diners on the Supperclub's trademark communal beds.

opposite
The all-black Bar Noir, with blue-tinted windows and snaking booth seating.

right
Farmyard-inspired forms
include cow-shaped stools
carved from oak.

opposite
The floor features illuminated
resin panels that change
colour as the evening
progresses.

Le Chlösterli /
Gstaad, Switzerland

Patrick Jouin, December 2003

French designer Patrick Jouin's partnership with global superchef Alain Ducasse continues apace with the creation of Le Spoon des neiges, a restaurant in the snowy, Alpine heights of Gstaad. The restaurant is part of a larger venue, Le Chlösterli, an ancient Swiss chalet, which also features a second, more traditional, restaurant-bar, an outdoor terrace and a nightclub, all designed by Jouin for a budget of approximately 6 million Euros ($7.8 million).

Built by monks of the Abbaye de Rougemont in 1721, Le Chlösterli was originally a farm that supplied goods to a nearby monastery in Saanen. In renovating the interior, Jouin took care to respect the eighteenth-century fabric of the building: 'We were surrounded by old things, so we didn't want to introduce anything fake. Everything is Swiss-made. We used stone, leather, glass – materials that age very well.'

The brief was two-fold. 'The owner Michel Pastor is a gourmand, and he wanted to have a Ducasse restaurant. His daughter Delphine wanted to have a nightclub and bar for a young crowd,' says Jouin. 'So the idea was a unification of different crowds and ambience in one place. We didn't want diners arriving at 8.00pm to feel as though they were in an empty nightclub, and we didn't want the

younger crowd to feel as though they were in a restaurant. So we played with the space; it's not really a restaurant and not really a nightclub. It's something different.'

Although the existing timber chalet shell remains, Jouin inserted modern elements into the lofty space. 'I wanted guests to know there is a good restaurant there, so we put in a big wall of glass that cuts the place in two. So you are surrounded by old wood, but you see through a modern wall into the clean, contemporary kitchen.' Le Spoon des neiges, on the first floor, and the chef's table are separated off by clear glazing and a wine wall, making them visible from the club area, where guests first arrive.

In the club, Jouin has taken his inspiration from Le Chlösterli's former life. Bringing the outside in, the floor features a pattern of stone paving, which is replicated on the large table tops that serve two group booths. The lighting system is integrated in the form of resin panels containing LEDs. 'It's like a Michael Jackson video. When you arrive, the colour is set to blue, so it's quite cold. When the DJ arrives later at 11 o'clock, the music volume increases, the atmosphere changes, and these lights become warmer in tone and more alive.'

Club furniture reveals whimsical dairy references: oak stools fashioned into bovine forms; milk pails that double up as champagne buckets; glowing, internally lit tables, with white Corian tops, disguised as giant timber buckets, full of milk; and oblong leather poufs that resemble bales of hay. Other pedestal tables are lit by hunks of crystal, 'like you find in the mountains'.

As Jouin says, 'Switzerland is a place so frozen in the past, it has a kind of perfection and can be quite serious. Yet it is also a place where you are meant to go on holiday and have fun. Le Chlösterli is a chic restaurant, but also a place to have fun, so we put some humour into it, creating the impression of a funky farm.'

above
Traditional materials of stone, timber and glass were used both inside and outside to create the clean exterior.

left
The first-floor restaurant Spoon is visible from the club below through the glazed wine wall.

above
Stone paving has also been
used on table tops.

above left
Club furniture resembles milk
pails and hay bales.

Shochu Lounge / London, UK

Super Potato, July 2004

Tokyo-based Super Potato is one of the most successful design agencies in Asia. Responsible for many retail, hotel and restaurant projects in their native country, they are also the creators of the functional, minimal aesthetic that defines the Muji brand. Recently, they have expanded to design restaurant interiors in the US and Europe. In 2002, Noriyoshi Muramatsu of Super Potato took their distinctive and simple organic style, favouring paper, timber and stone, to London to create the Zuma restaurant.

　　Two years later, they returned to design the sequel, Roka, which includes the Shochu Lounge below. Shochu, an ancient spirit distilled from raw produce, such as sweet potato or buckwheat, and then flavoured with fruits and herbs, is growing in popularity in Japan, with many specialist bars springing up in Tokyo. Shochu Lounge is understood to be the first such bar in Europe. It is accessible from a separate entrance next to Roka, on a lively Fitzrovia street, lined with restaurants and bars.

above
Red fabric strips adorn the wall in one lounge area.

In his quest for authenticity, Muramatsu has taken the drink as inspiration, integrating the artefacts and promoting the rituals involved in producing and serving the spirit. Taking centre stage is an L-shaped bar, topped by a roughly hewn, 270-year-old elm counter, and accompanied by chunky bar stools. Behind the staff service area is a lower communal table, where guests can sit and watch the bartender chip pieces off a giant block of ice, frozen in such a way as to be crystal clear.

Antique timber artefacts, including barrels and buckets, sourced from an old distillery, are mounted to form a 3-D collage and backdrop to the bar action. Elsewhere, the flavoured Shochu becomes part of the decoration, with huge, squat glass jars, displaying their fruity infusions, sitting in square niches of a large floor-to-ceiling timber shelving unit. The basement space is lent a rustic warmth by the earthenware textured walls, the heavy use of timber and copper (such as copper-framed standard lamps and a large copper wall panel) and the splashes of bright-red patchwork fabric.

There are two pockets of lounge seating, one raised and furnished with chairs and sofas, upholstered in the red patchwork cloth, which is repeated as a vibrant wall covering in the other area. Arranged horizontally, the lengthy strips of fabric are up-lit to highlight their raw threads and torn edges, against which black sofas and chairs, bearing a black bamboo-patterned upholstery, strike a contrast. By reinterpreting an ancient tradition, respecting Japanese heritage and through the use of natural materials, Super Potato have created an interior infused with the Shochu spirit in the heart of twenty-first-century London.

below left
Natural materials, such as the chunky 270-year-old elmwood bar, create a rustic warmth.

plan
The two seating lounges are next to the central bar and adjoining low, communal shochu table.

Chapter Three: *Hotel Bars*

above
The wine-tasting table and glass wine-wall storage in Dionisio wine bar.

above
L'Angelo lounge has zebra-print-upholstered chairs, with traditional Venetian frames, featuring figurines.

plan, opposite
Both bars are located off the lobby, on the ground floor of the hotel. 1. entrance, 2. lobby, 3. reception, 4. L'Angelo lounge bar, 5. Dionisio wine bar, 6. restaurant, 7. kitchen

L'Angelo Lounge Bar and Dionisio Wine Bar, Aleph Hotel / Rome, Italy

Tihany Design, May 2003

Drinking in L'Angelo lounge bar or Dionisio wine bar, in Rome's Aleph Hotel, is meant to feel like hell. The American architect Adam D. Tihany, a prolific restaurant and hotel designer, took his inspiration from Dante's *Divine Comedy* when creating the interior of this five-star boutique hotel. Paradise is promised in the cellar spa, but the ground-floor public areas are clearly inferno-themed, with fiery, devilish red as the dominant colour.

The two neighbouring bars are located off the main lobby and situated en route to the Sin restaurant. L'Angelo is the more decadent, with Padouk-wood panelling and a highly polished, black granite floor, inset with a geometric pattern in red Bisazza mosaic tiles. The glossy finishes continue above, with the ceiling composition of lacquered, circular discs. Furniture is a mixture of red, leather-upholstered sofas, zebra-print chairs, with carved-timber frames featuring typically Venetian figurines (reproductions by Giovanni Monzio Compagnoni), and mirrored tables resembling giant dice, lending the lounge a hint of Bacchanalian debauchery.

The centrepiece is a simple, white Corian bar, with a lower façade of red glass, accompanied by red leather stools. Behind this, a free-standing unit, with a white front and mirrored sides houses, bar equipment and provides work space for the bartenders. Two vertical strips, containing LED lights, run down its side, displaying rude messages in Italian.

Adjoining this space is the smaller, wood-panelled Dionisio wine bar, which features a display of glasses and wine storage, a large T-shaped tasting table and three side tables, which extend from wall niches. The T-shaped table takes centre stage, emphasized by the rectangle of red mosaic flooring, upon which it stands. The table top is decorated with a silk-screen of an old workshop table, and is protected by glass and illuminated by several Ingo Maurer lamps. Dramatic photographic artworks by New York food stylist and artist Nir Adar were commissioned for the walls.

Since red not only symbolizes passion and lust, but is also said to promote hunger, perhaps denizens of Dionisio will find themselves drawn towards Sin, the restaurant beyond.

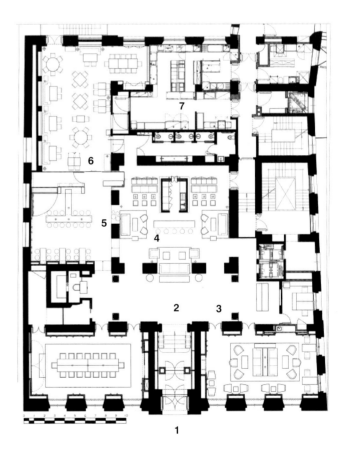

Happy Bar, Hi Hotel / Nice, France

matali crasset, March 2003

matali crasset's Happy Bar, at Nice's 38-room Hi
Hotel, makes design on a budget look like candy-
coloured child's play. The Paris-based product and
furniture designer is a 'petite enfant de Starck',
and, like other Starck protégés, Christophe Pillet
and Patrick Jouin, has now flown the nest to reach
her own stellar heights. In 1997, she received the
Paris Grand Prix du Design, and, one year later,
established her own studio in the French capital.

Designing an entire hotel was a stimulating
challenge for crasset. 'It's global, a real hotel
with music, image, art,' she says. 'It is interesting
because it is like making a never-ending object
which you use and then see how it can be changed
from day to day' (www.designboom.com). The
hoteliers, Patrick Elouarghi and Philippe Chapelet,
asked her to 'Change things. Throw out the hotel
typology' (*Frame* No. 34, Sept/Oct 2003).

For the dining-room-cum-bar area, crasset
responded to the brief by inserting a ribbed
capsule, made from birch plywood, into the double-
height space. This installation houses chartreuse
leatherette-upholstered banquettes, forming a cosy
enclosure for drinkers. A narrow mezzanine, with a
fuchsia resin floor, runs the length of the room.

This accommodates bookshelves and seating, including crasset's distinctive, upright 'Capuce' armchairs (manufactured by Domodinamica). It is also where the DJs play at night.

Additional plywood furniture, in bright shades of apple green, fuchsia and sky blue, litter the space like children's toys or building blocks. These simple pieces are multi-purpose; table tops transform into shelves when slotted into the wall, and rectangular ottomans function as poofs or tables. Everything is designed for easy storage (tables fit beneath the banquettes) and mobility, with handles built into each unit. The felt-tip palette of the Happy Bar resonates throughout the hotel, from the clean façade, punctuated by windows bathed in various hues, to the guestrooms, bursting with colour.

By night, the bar exudes a more clubby vibe. Coloured lighting drenches the space in warm pinks; a video screen descends, playing host to dynamic visuals; and international DJs, such as Laurent Garnier and Galliano, frequently entertain the Happy crowd.

above
Additional seating includes crasset's 'Capuce' dining chairs.

opposite left
View from the mezzanine gallery, which is furnished with book shelves and seating.

opposite right
A ribbed plywood capsule contains banquette seating.

above
The bar is dominated by
the red and black coils of
Cappellini's AND sofas.

Bar, UNA Hotel Vittoria / Florence, Italy

Fabio Novembre, June 2003

Fabio Novembre has produced some dazzling gems, most notably Café L'Atlantique nightclub, and the restaurant and bar Shu (see *Bar and Club Design*), both in Milan. This passionate Italian, part-poet, part-philosopher, urges everyone to 'be your own messiah'. Inspired by love and life itself, his emotive creations are flamboyant gestures that often disrupt convention and seek to captivate the heart.

Novembre tackled the UNA Hotel, his first hotel project, with characteristically playful verve. He believes that 'the hotel is a trailer for the movie that the city is going to show you' (*Frame* No. 37, March/April 2004). Thus, his interiors for this Tuscan villa draw on Florentine traditions, and on the Medici era in particular because he is fascinated by the interplay of light and shadow: 'A mutable theatre of shadows, offspring of mystical opacity is the condition I try to create in my works.'

Novembre believes that successful social spaces are essentially sets, created to seduce. The beauty of the UNA Hotel Vittoria is that the façade has remained unchanged, so that when guests step inside they are delighted by the villa's fairytale magic. Spellbound, they are instantly transported by Novembre's floral-mosaic 'carpet' (Opus Romano by Bisazza), which curls from over their heads down to the floor, towards the reception desk. It is this form that is repeated in the adjoining lobby bar.

Here, as much art installation as furniture, two looping, red-and-black coils – AND sofas manufactured by Cappellini – cocoon drinkers in tunnels of love. Reminiscent of Verner Panton's all-enveloping designs, each sofa is like unravelling head-over-heels hearts, completed by a full-stop of 'LOVE' – black, glass-topped tables, modelled on Robert Indiana's iconic pop-art print.

Novembre's bespoke pieces are cradled by the curling floor, by Tino Sana, which arches up to meet the bar at one end and becomes the ceiling above, echoing the loopy forms of the sofas and foyer. Spotlights, recessed between the ceiling panels, emphasize the sculptural quality of the sofas and create striking contrasts of light and shadow.

UNA Hotel Vittoria's bar is both innovative and traditional. Novembre says that, deep down, inside he is very baroque and his work will always be 'unavoidably Italian', so, from possibly the most romantic culture in the world, here's a bar that encourages patrons to get comfortably loved-up.

left
Novembre's flamboyant mosaic decorates the reception lobby.

below left
One of the Robert Indiana-inspired LOVE tables.

Q! Hotel Bar / Berlin, Germany

GRAFT, April 2004

Seeking to challenge the 'museum typology' of the hotel interior, progressive, young architecture team GRAFT conceived a new, futuristic landscape for Berlin's Q! Hotel. Walls slope into floors, and vertical surfaces loop and undulate, creating various planes that function as furniture and light sources. Thomas Willemeit of GRAFT refers to this as the 'hybridization of space', where elements blend with each other to become multifunctional, or, at least, ambiguous. 'Therefore, guests change their interaction with furniture and architecture, and become the actors on the lifestyle stage,' says Willemeit.

Q! is situated on the corner of a side street, just off the Kurfürstendamm in Charlottenburg. All 76 rooms, spa and ground-floor cocktail bar and restaurant were created by GRAFT, a multi-disciplinary architectural firm that was established in 1998 by Willemeit, Lars Krückeberg and Wolfram Putz. The trio have offices in Berlin and Los Angeles (with a Bejing base on the way), and have, so far, received most attention for their LA residential projects, developed jointly with film actor Brad Pitt. The arrival of Q! Hotel, however, looks set to change this.

Promoted by the hotel as the 'core element and pulsating heart of Q!', the dark-red bar is clearly visible from the street. It appears to have been sculpted from a flowing horizontal that shelters the reception area, and which slants diagonally down to form the lounge, with various protrusions and indentations providing seating nooks and platforms. Designed using CAD, the timber construction was machine-cut according to the computer measurements by a carpenter and fitted together like a puzzle. The red, structured Marmoleum skin gives it a cohesive, smooth finish.

left
The interior is covered in a
Marmoleum skin to give
a cohesive finish.

opposite top
The glowing Q! is clearly
visible from the street.

opposite bottom
The bar itself has a façade
of back-lit acid-etched glass.

Willemeit says, 'Our initial inspiration was the way the Japanese sit low on the floor, "grafted" with the idea of a commune; we wanted to make the space accessible and erase boundaries, like the way we melt the reception with the lobby. So the hotel becomes a stage set, an atmosphere and a background that offers drama.' Drinkers are cradled in this considered environment, which has been likened to a flying carpet and an 'upscale red skateboard park' (*Sleeper*, Issue 1, Autumn 2004).

Back-lit acid-etched glass panels, integrated into the bar, and the voids created by the jutting shelves and sloping platforms, together with a fire, recessed low into the only vertical section, light the interior. Bespoke, asymmetrical sofas echo the dynamic angles of the interior shell, melding with the distorted horizontal, so that the walls become part of the furniture.

Although open to residents, the bar is members-only, with its own separate entrance. White drapes, suspended from a recessed curtain track, can be drawn across the glazed façade, allowing guests to shield themselves from prying eyes and to maintain a sense of chi-chi cocktail-lounge exclusivity.

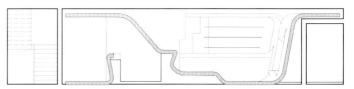

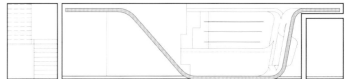

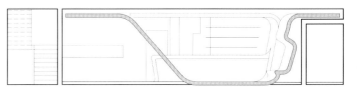

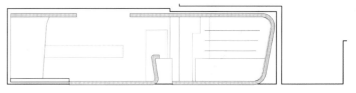

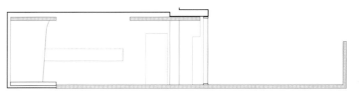

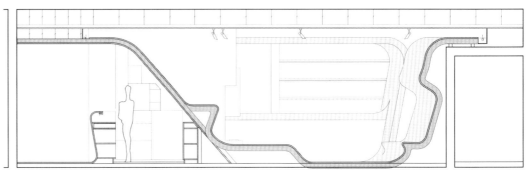

above
GRAFT 'melted' the floors into the walls to create a communal 'stage set' for guests.

plan
Sections through different points in the bar show the various indentations and sloping planes that form Q!

Hotel Derlon Bar / Maastricht, Netherlands

SEVV, September 2003

Studio Edward van Vliet (SEVV) looked to the east for inspiration when designing the champagne-cocktail lounge at the Hotel Derlon. The Amsterdam-based, multidisciplinary design agency was asked to transform the ground floor and basement of this small 44-roomed hotel, located in the buzzing, old city centre of Maastricht. Their renovation comprises the new Zes restaurant on the ground floor, crowned by grand square chandeliers of brushed steel and glass rods, and this intimate, 100 square metre (1,075 square foot) lounge below.

'The inspiration was Marco Polo,' says van Vliet, 'the famous Italian who travelled to Asia in the thirteenth century and brought back unfamiliar riches to Europe. Whereas the restaurant is decorated in an Italian style, combined with Asian details, the cocktail lounge is predominantly Asian-inspired.' Several elements combine to generate an eastern aura, not least the low, Japanese-style seating levels, simple minimalist tables, and, perhaps most significantly, the geometric floral pattern that has been applied to yin-and-yang effect.

Chunky, low bespoke 'fauteuils', upholstered in chenille, bear this distinctive pattern in light-beige relief against a black background. This is then reversed in the laser-cut metal of the frosted acrylate panels that surround the space. As these twenty-first-century versions of ornate, antique screens are dramatically back-lit to glow various, changing hues, from apple green to sunset orange and midnight blue, the pattern is thrown into silhouette (as opposed to light), thus rendering it the negative to the positive motif of the chairs.

The low seating levels, indirect, diffuse lighting and interplay of light and shadow all work to enhance the sense of space. Red carpeting and cushions add warmth and internally lit, white acrylate tables provide a glamorous glow. Access to the bar is via a lift or marble-lined Mediterranean-travertine stairs. However, all internal walls and stairs are obscured and softened by diaphanous white drapes, reinforcing the illusion of infinite space. Since opening, this champagne-cocktail lounge has become a hotspot for discerning locals and has prompted the refurbishment of the hotels 44 guest rooms.

above
Back-lit patterned screens enhance the sense of space.

opposite
Mediterranean-travertine-lined stairs lead down from the lobby to the bar.

Hotel Derlon Bar

Chapter Four: *Clubs*

190east / Frankfurt, Germany
....
Kay Mack + Partner, August 2000

above
The white furnishings of the
Chill-Out Lounge are warmed
up by red cushions and pink
back-lit panels.

When it comes to the gentrification of derelict docks and disused industrial wastelands, bar and club operators are often the pioneers, taking advantage of empty warehouses and crumbling lofts, where rents are cheap and space plentiful. Such inventive opportunism occurs relentlessly, from London's Shoreditch to Lisbon's docks, from Berlin's Mitte to New York's Meatpacking District or the Lower East Side. It is in this spirit that 190east was born. The club is located in a former brewery in what was a redundant industrial zone on the east side of Frankfurt. Today, the area is a cocktail of night-time venues, start-up companies, ad agencies and the likes of Jaguar and BMW.

The DJ-owner's brief to local architect Kay Mack was based on the TV series *Shaft*. He was asked to transform the idea of a 1970s New York club into a modern, designed space. The result is very millennial, with cream vinyl-upholstered furniture and integrated lighting elements combined with exposed brick, lending the venue a space-age, industrial feel. Ergonomic curves ease the flow of patrons and are also reminiscent of the retro-futuro aesthetic of the 1960s and 1970s.

190east occupies a basement measuring 380 square metres (4,090 square feet), which Mack has divided into three areas: the main club and dance floor, and adjoining Ocean Bar and Chill-Out Lounge. There is also a record store on the premises, although it is closed at night, when it functions as the cloakroom. An inclusive atmosphere is created for patrons in the main club by a series of low booths that line the wall opposite the bar. Here, the yellow, back-lit bar and lighting installations, mounted in wall recesses, generate warmth and the illusion of depth. Fixed, oval illuminated tables provide additional surface space for standing drinkers. They also guide clubbers towards the dance floor, which is set aglow by a wall of beaming 'mini suns' that alter for discotastic light shows.

The other spaces are defined by contrasting accent colours. Patrons can opt for the cool blues of the Ocean Bar or the warm pinks and reds of the Chill-Out Lounge. Flexible, low stools, upholstered in blue vinyl, and similarly mobile, internally illuminated tables allow for changeable seating formations in the Ocean Bar.

The Chill-Out Lounge, conversely, is all about reclining across scarlet cushions, strewn about simple white, curved benches, which are fixed around a central, oval seating island to create a more intimate enclosure. With its late-night lounging and light-fantastic dance floor, 190east has created a new design currency in Germany's financial capital.

above left
Ergonomic curves lend the main bar a retro-futuristic feel.

left
Small stools in the Ocean Bar allow for flexible seating arrangements.

Red Cat Club / Mainz, Germany

Timpe + Wendling, August 2002

Timpe + Wendling's renovation of Mainz's Red Cat Club is testament to the fact that economic restrictions often generate unusual, innovative design. This subterranean club first opened in 1999 and occupies three barrel-vaulted cellars that previously belonged to a wine merchant. Inspiration for the initial concept was derived from 1960s and 1970s R&B, soul, funk and disco culture, even though the venue also plays host to contemporary electronic dance music.

'Such musical diversity is reflected in the eclectic, playful and often improvised interior that is not taking itself too seriously,' say Timpe + Wendling, who refer to the Red Cat Club's interior-design style as 'DIY LoFi'. The existing club consisted of a discothèque and bar, the latter decked out in opulent-meets-industrial materials of dark-red velvet, faux-marble columns and golden ornamentation, which was juxtaposed with a concrete bar counter.

Timpe + Wendling were commissioned to revamp the disco and to create a new lounge in the third connecting vault, previously used as a chill-out space. The brief asked that the designers provide a 'harmonious enhancement to the existing style, rather than contrasting, or changing it'. With only 75,000 Euros ($97,000), Timpe + Wendling set to work, paying specific attention to 'spatial transition, discovery and identity of spaces.'

Where patrons descend from the bar into the disco vault, Timpe + Wendling inserted a platform, furnished with bespoke seating and tables at either end: 'this provides orientation, or withdrawal and rest, from the action on the dance floor.' These seating pockets are set against custom-designed, retro wallpaper, adding a sense of 1970s-flavoured home comfort, in contrast to the rough texture of the stone walls.

The simple furniture here is used throughout the venue; low, movable benches, with foam upholstery and angled metal legs, sit with occasional tables of ash timber with integrated lighting, pale-green linoleum tops and golden rims. The lamps bear a variety of shades, from leopard print to gingham – think domestic 1950s furniture with a twist. For dancing patrons' drink disposal, a series of curved, wooden panels on slender, steel legs twists along the walls in the discothèque.

The arched passageway leading from the disco to the lounge is draped in ceiling-to-floor brown-cord curtain, shrouding clubbers on their way to the second bar. The lounge is Timpe + Wendling's tour de force: the bar is sheltered by a canopy, sculpted to follow the curvature of the vault. This grey gypsum-board layer arches up and over the ceiling, hiding technical services, such as air ducts, as well as recessed lighting. Tessellated panelwork, comprising orange and grey recycled canteen trays, defines the bar itself, rendering it the warm, hearth-like focus of the lounge. A giant Persian rug, protected by perspex, wraps around the MDF bar counter, enriching this effect.

Timpe + Wendling's artful, unconventional solutions make for a unique, whimsical space – just their intention: 'by sampling and super-imposing different influences and styles, we've gone beyond polished retro styles. Identity is not a question of "pureness" and we hope that it will make people think beyond the limits of "style".'

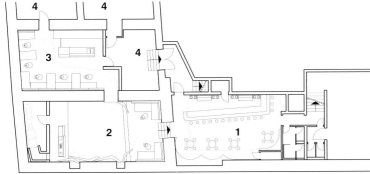

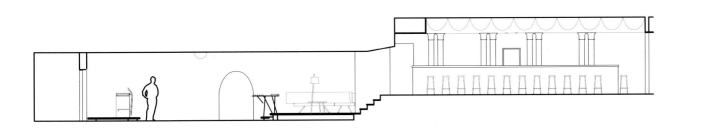

above
Specially designed furniture includes 1950s-style tables with integrated lamps.

plan
1. bar, 2. disco, 3. lounge, 4. storage

section
Long section through the club, showing the different levels.

opposite left
One of the seating areas overlooking the dance floor, with custom-designed wallpaper.

opposite right
Recycled plastic trays create a canopy over the bar.

Jimmy Woo / Amsterdam, Netherlands

B.inc design, December 2003

above
Oriental-design screens and orchids set an eastern tone.

above right
The opium bed is set against a gold-leaf wall, adorned with erotic Araki photographs.

opposite
Seating platforms feature a mixture of antique furniture and modern-day pieces.

Amsterdam's boutique club Jimmy Woo is a pedigree hybrid, mixing authentic, antique Asian elements with cutting-edge twenty-first-century disco bling. It is the third venue in the city to be opened by local, pioneering bar-and-club entrepreneur Casper Reinders, and the second with an Oriental theme. His cocktail bar, Suzy Wongs, opened in the summer of 2002, and proved so popular that he decided to develop the concept further, just across the street.

Still looking to the east for inspiration, Jimmy Woo was designed by Eric Kuster of B.inc design in the style of the home of a sociable Chinese businessman from Hong Kong, who enjoys throwing decadent parties. Hence the virtually anonymous entrance, with just a small name-plate announcing the venue's presence. Beyond this, Reinders's ambition was to create the very best club. 'The idea was simple,' he says. 'To open a club that was according to my own standards of extremely high quality – hence the Funktion-One sound system – and could rival anything in London or New York.'

Upon arrival, patrons ascend a stairway and pass through large copper doors, adorned by an etched portrait of an Asian face, to reach the cocktail lounge. Nineteenth-century antiques, including an opium bed overlooked by Araki photographs of girls trussed up in bondage, are showcased on illuminated seating platforms. These are enclosed by black voile drapes and black screens, bearing a simple geometric pattern repeated elsewhere in the scheme.

A keen antiques collector, Reinders says 'I don't really like very contemporary things, but prefer something with character and soul, which is why we used genuine antiques in Jimmy Woo. I think it really adds soul to the place.' Surrounding walls gleam with gold leaf, and the long bar is bathed in mauve light, which radiates from the back-lit glass panels of the back bar.

Meanwhile, downstairs the atmosphere changes radically. Project manager Erjan Borren says, 'When you go downstairs, you feel like you're going into the basement. We created a more underground feel with an unfinished oak floor, metal and fabric walls, and, of course, the ceiling with the lights.' Reinders was inspired to install a canopy of bulbs over the dance floor by the dazzling backdrop (created by lighting director Michael Keeler) in Justin Timberlake's 'Rock Your Body' video.

Lighting wizard Andras Pollé realized Reinders's dream by creating a $190,000 Digital Matrix panel installation, comprising 12,000 4-watt tungsten lightbulbs. Controlled by 3,000 DMX channels, these possess the capacity to flash, dim and strobe. 'My philosophy is that LEDs are not sexy, because they can project a cold light,' explains Pollé. 'However, an ordinary lightbulb contains the full range of the colour spectrum. When dimmed, they turn red, and that makes them sexy as hell.' His custom-designed system (called Lucifer, after the angel of light) allows a tight control of light output and temperature.

Computer programmers are currently devising intelligent software to enable even more impressive effects. 'Each group of four lamps will be controllable, like one pixel. This will mean we can create waterfalls, fireballs, images and scrolling text. You can make the entire ceiling twinkle, or hit you hard like a strobe-scope.' Pollé envisages even more 'crazy' and spectacular lighting for Reinders's forthcoming New York club: Jimmy Woo is set to take Manhattan in 2005.

left
Jimmy Woo's custom-designed lighting system, called Lucifer, after the angel of light, can produce endless dazzling effects.

Divina Disco / Milan, Italy

Fabio Novembre, October 2001

Fabio Novembre's creations are always spectacular, and the Divina Disco in Milan is no exception. It may not possess the star quality of his Café L'Atlantique, also in Milan, with its heavenly shower chandelier of fibre-optic tentacles, but it certainly features some sights to behold. Behind every Novembre project lies a myth or love story; inspiration for this erotic night club, or 'temple of femininity', as the man himself describes it, came from the name of the old, pre-existing venue: Divina.

'Personally, I've always been amazed by the fact that a woman gives birth,' says Novembre. 'Men are creators of things, women are creators of life. The perception of it has brought many sensible men (artists) to the divinization of the woman. The naked female body is pure essence. Exploring its secrets opens the doors of perception. Relating to its beauty makes you adore it.' Divina Disco is Novembre's homage to woman in all her naked glory, 'filtered through the classicity of 500 years of art history, through the elegance of ageless, visionary adorers'.

A womblike entrance, with red velvet-lined walls and an undulating mirror-tiled ceiling, opens out into the 300 square metre (3,250 square foot) club. At the heart is a circular dance floor, made of glass mosaic tiles by Bisazza and crowned by a reflective, silver dome, with spotlights. Reminiscent of an art gallery, surrounding walls are punctuated with seating recesses and display digital prints, on Trevira material, of various reclining female nudes by Old Masters, such as Mussini, Boucher, Grosso, Giorgione, Ingres and Velàzquez. Divans, on which guests can recline, if they wish, in the same recumbent poses of the nude women, become part of the paintings.

above
A mosaic of Courbet's painting arches up from behind the bar over the heads of drinkers.

opposite
Seating niches display recumbent nudes by Old Masters.

overleaf
A circular dance floor, made of Bisazza mosaic, is crowned by a radiant silver dome.

Stepping up to the bar, patrons are confronted by Divina Disco's *pièce de résistance*, a colossal mosaic reproducing Gustave Courbet's 1866 painting of the genitalia of a recumbent woman, *L'Origine du monde*. The image is visible to those seated on the perimeter of the dance floor and is positioned to 'quench the thirst of dancing guests' and arches up to form the ceiling directly above the bar area, thus enveloping drinkers. Novembre produced this 'interactive' gallery, where the paintings are almost literally part of the furniture, in the hope that guests get inside the paintings and feel the images physically, to 'elevate the souls and stimulate the bodies'.

The erotic imagery lays bare the hedonistic and sexually charged atmosphere of the discothèque, in which dancing can be considered a courtship-cum-mating ritual. As well as displaying man's worship of the female form, the artworks also serve to remind the viewer of the voyeurism that is the lifeblood of nightclubs. Like it or not (would John Berger and certain feminists approve?), the Divina Disco is a characteristically provocative Novembre response to the request for something 'divine'.

left
A circular dance floor, made
of Bisazza mosaic, is crowned
by a radiant silver dome.

Helsinki Club / Helsinki, Finland

Anteeksi Allstars, March 2003

Breathing new life into a beloved 30-year-old nightclub and casino is a daunting task, no matter how faded it may be. The Helsinki Club, a local legend in the Finnish capital, was in dire need of a twenty-first-century overhaul. Design firm M41LH2 joined forces with the design agency com-pa-ny and designers Tuomas Kivinen, Selina Anttinen and Vesa Oiva to form the Anteeksi Allstars, a design collective created specifically to undertake the revamp.

The Anteeksi Allstars were commissioned 'to make the club attractive again and restore its past glory as an international-level quality venue, within a minimum amount of time and budget'. On a more practical level, they were asked to disrupt the circulation system to create a desired crowding in certain areas of the venue. To excite and intrigue patrons, who visit the Helsinki Club to drink, dance or gamble, a series of different atmospheres and moods was established within the 800-person-capacity space (which covers 750 square metres (8,100 square feet)) by treating each area as a distinctly separate entity. The result is a rich, vibrant tableau of contrasts, unified, however, by quirky detailing and a daringly florid use of colour, light and pattern.

The entrance ramp leads patrons into an ethereal bar, crowned by a light-filled cupola that bathes the room in pulsating hues of orange, yellow and green. From one corner, a peninsula bar projects into the space; seating is provided by bespoke high tables and velvet-upholstered Select Bar chairs by Harri Korhonen for Inno. Naive tree cut-outs, silhouetted by hidden back-lighting, animate the bar, lending it a certain depth.

right
The first bar, with its lit cupola that moves through various hues.

opposite
Main circulation route, furnished with tram seats.

In stark contrast to this relatively sparse, airy environment is the neighbouring central lounge, a gaudy, raised enclosure, with an excessive, baroque-patterned interior. Wall-to-wall carpeting is taken to the limit here: simple, custom-designed benches and some of the walls are wrapped in a custom-made wool fabric, which bears a dramatic Versace-on-acid motif. Traditional Finnish wallpaper makes a comeback on the ceiling and remaining walls, with the shiny surfaces of tray-tables, sunken into the bench tops, reflecting its ornate flourishes. The effect, for those lounging, is of being in a heady, three-dimensional swirl of pattern.

Windows overlooking the adjoining bar and sunken dance floor afford some visual relief. It was here that the Anteeksi Allstars made considerable alterations, demolishing the existing structural elements to make way for the new bar, stage, DJ booth and air-conditioning, plus the new steel-and-glass stairway, mezzanine balcony and VIP area (separated by a red glazed partition).

Fittingly, this throbbing heart of the Helsinki Club is awash with energizing colours of red and orange. Against fiery, sunset hues, the brilliant-white bar (with its stainless-steel counters and flush lighting from the top) is an appealing prospect for sweaty clubbers. Freestanding subwoofer-speaker units define the dance floor and offer elevated surfaces for podium dancers. Above the glass ceiling is an attic space, housing eight high-powered strobelights. 'This can make the entire ceiling flash extremely brightly in time to the music. It looks really cool,' say Anteeksi Allstars. Patrons can survey the red-hot action below from the comfort of the mezzanine, which is furnished with fixed, internally lit cocktail tables.

right
The main lounge overlooking the dance floor, with its Versace-on-acid, baroque interior.

128   Chapter 4: Clubs

The small casino is fairly standard, aside from the bespoke wallpaper, whose pattern is identical to that on the central-lounge carpet, and the resin-cast floor, which contains genuine Euro 5 cent coins. The Anteeksi Allstars' treatment of the main circulation route, a corridor that runs the length of the dance floor and lounge, is somewhat more inspiring. 'We turned it into a tramway tunnel, installing seats and tables that are standard issue in Helsinki public transport authority trams.' Gentle lighting emanates from beneath the seats, and an orange striped carpet covers the walls, creating a welcoming rendezvous zone, which seems to stretch for miles beyond the mirrored end walls. All in all, Helsinki Club looks destined to be a disco inferno for some time to come.

right
The pure white bar (to the left) provides a soothing contrast to the hot red shades of the dance floor area.

Chapter 4: Clubs

Cielo / New York, USA

Dupoux Design, December 2002

Multi-award-winning 'boutique club' Cielo is Stephane Dupoux's first Manhattan project. The French-born designer made his name amongst the chic party elite, creating cool *boîtes*, such as Pearl, Touch and Nikki Beach, in Miami's South Beach.

Cielo is located in the equally hip destination-location of New York's Meatpacking District. The concept was inspired by the owners, Nicolas Matar, an internationally known DJ, and Philippe Rieser, after their many years on the nightclub circuit. 'Our vision was to create a timelessly chic, yet futuristic, nightclub, with a sexy and intimate feel,' says Matar. They asked Dupoux to 'orientate the design towards music and dancing'. The result is a cosy, flashing beat-box, where house music and dancing reigns.

'My initial idea was the recording studio,' explains Dupoux. 'I wanted to produce the very best sound quality, hence the padded walls. Secondly, I wanted to give it an amphitheatre feel, so I created a central, sunken dance floor; the dance floor is the entertainment.' Matar installed an unparalleled sound system, made by Funktion-One. DJs rule over the 300-capacity space from a mosaic-clad booth, overlooking the dance floor.

Cielo is a prime example of the trend towards cosier, more intimate nightclub spaces; it is only 270 square metres (3,000 square feet). As Dupoux says, 'I wanted Cielo to feel safe and cosy, to counteract all the anxiety in the world.' The idea of rural escapism is one of the influences here: 'I wanted to instil the feel of a mountain cabin, that cosiness.' Instead of timber logs, Dupoux lined the interior with Ultrasuede-covered foam logs, in several shades of brown. 'Everything is done for a reason. The Ultrasuede is darker at banquette level, then grows lighter and then darker again, as it reaches the ceiling, to give the feeling of infinity in quite a confined space. That's a very unusual feeling.' The soft, plush logs are interspersed with back-lit perspex tubes.

These parallel lines of light are connected to the DJ booth, and blink to the beat, making the entire club pulsate with sound and light. Mirrors enhance the visual effect ad infinitum.

A window overlooking a small, exotic garden patio (for smokers) reduces the risk of cabin fever. Cielo has been described in one American club magazine as a 'retro-Euro interpretation of Tron, only in this game, the players wear Prada.' Judging by its success, for New York clubbers there's no doubt that Cielo means heaven.

opposite
Ultrasuede padded 'logs', in a range of shades of brown, give the 'feeling of infinity'.

below
In the raised seating areas, low bar tables feature sunken bottle-holders.

Chapter 4: Clubs

Avalon / New York, USA

Desgrippes Gobé Group, September 2003

A legend in its own lifetime, New York's Limelight club opened in the late 1970s in a large, neogothic Episcopalian church, dating back to the 1840s. Like all the best clubs, it catered to a diverse crowd, from students to stars. Straight and gay clubbers mixed in the hedonistic atmosphere of the halcyon days of house music in the 1980s, ingesting drugs and dancing until dawn.

  The party ended tragically. In 1996, Limelight promoter Michael Alig was convicted of murdering Angel Melendez, a drug dealer who frequented the club. This grim tale is immortalized in James St. James's novel *Disco Bloodbath* and in the subsequent film *Party Monster*. When Limelight owner Peter Gatien was jailed for income-tax evasion three years later, the club's fate was sealed. In order for the 1500-person-capacity venue to survive, 'it was in need of a serious sleaze exorcism, not to mention a design redemption' (*Interior Design*, January 2003).

  Desgrippes Gobé Group stepped in as saviours of the iconic Chelsea nightspot, resurrecting it for the twenty-first century. 'When it first opened, the idea of dancing in a church was risqué and cool,' explains Head of Retail Design Sam O'Donahue. 'But since then, we've had Madonna's "Like a Prayer" video and the sacrilegious thing is passé.' Desgrippes Gobé removed the pseudo-spiritual paraphernalia and shoddy gothic elements. 'We decided to play down the religion and honour the beautiful original architecture,' says O'Donahue. Renovation of the 1,440 square metre (16,000 square foot), triple-level interior cost approximately $7.5 million, a large proportion of the sum being spent on replacing floors, the roof and rebuilding the property to make it safe.

left
Internally lit, frosted acrylic paving and back-lit stained glass illuminate the entrance to Avalon.

opposite
Guests pay at the bank of tills in the orange aperture, which is framed by contrasting cyan walls.

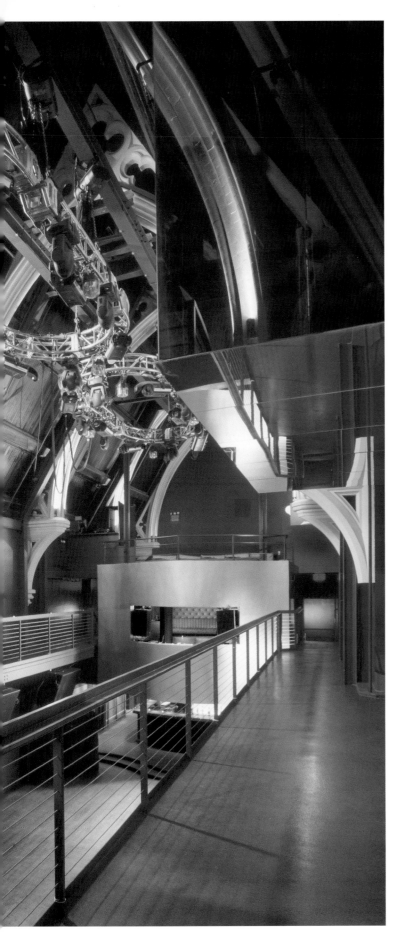

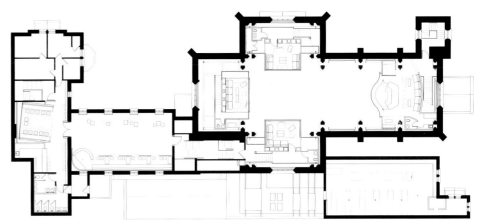

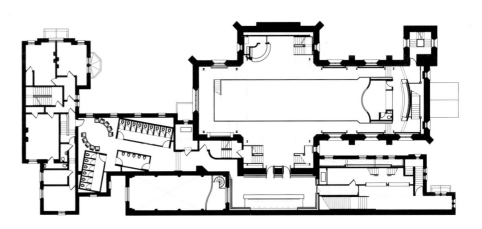

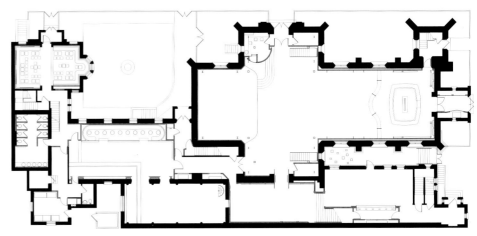

left
VIP mirrored cubes are suspended above the dance floor.

opposite
The Library bar, with a bottle display of mirror-backed shelves, enhances the sense of space and the gothic architecture.

plans
From bottom: ground, first and upper levels.

opposite
The Library bar, from another angle, showing its back-lit parchment-behind-acrylic counter.

below
A padded lounge enclosure provides a comfortable nook juxtaposed with the building's original features.

The labyrinthine character of the church was a challenge, but Desgrippes Gobé used this to their advantage. 'The building was developed over many years. There was no master plan. So the way that one space joins another is very circuitous. Although this meant it needed tidying up, it also gave us the opportunity to create an adventure, with several different experiences and areas.'

Reincarnated as Avalon, the club is organized into five thematic zones: Escape, Seduction, Fantasy, Energy and Discovery. The dance floors represent Energy, the lounges and VIP areas are classified as Escape, the bars and second-floor restrooms embody Seduction, the 'weird, in-between worlds', such as the Garden room (featuring faux topiary and fibre-optic lights, like stars) and first-floor restrooms, are Fantasy, and the entrance lobby and corridors symbolize Discovery: 'These are like a sorbet, cleansing your palate as you move from one experience to the next,' says O'Donahue.

Instant drama is guaranteed from the start. An entrance of illuminated, frosted cast-acrylic floor-paving lights the way and accentuates the existing stone walls and stained-glass window. Guests are immediately enveloped by a smooth, curved structure, spray-painted cyan, beneath which a bank of cash registers are clearly defined, set within an orange-hued, horizontal aperture. Throughout Avalon, these thoroughly modern finishes of bold colours and glittering surfaces, combined with space-age capsule forms, continue to be juxtaposed with the old.

The cruciform nave remains the heart of the club. Here, the dance floor is crowned by soaring gothic vaulting, painted white and spotlit. At one end of the space, the stage has been enlarged to cater for events, while, at the opposite end, the bar has been raised a few steps higher and given a polished, glossy look with a red, poured epoxy-resin floor. Avalon's bars are glitzy altars devoted to alcohol; this

ground-floor bar, overlooking the dance floor, has a twinkling counter of polyester-resin matrix, embedded with glass and aventurine-quartz chips. Surrounding walls are brightened by lime-tinted mirrors.

Elsewhere, the Library bar features a stunning bottle display of mirror-backed shelves, framed by the arch of a vaulting rib. The bar counter below is faced with back-lit parchment behind acrylic, which glows gold from a distance. In another of the venue's bars, cigarette-paper-thin, glinting aluminium, used in the manufacture of car frames, has been adapted to clad the walls and bar counter, which, lit from beneath, appears to float.

The DJs are the high-priests at Avalon, and those playing in the nave look out over their dancing flock from a second-floor booth. Up here, there is also a mini-lounge, with stadium-style tiers of seating for groupies, plus an en-suite toilet. VIPs hover at celestial heights in mirrored cubes, just below the church's ceiling beams. The cubes' physical imposition is lessened by the reflection on their surfaces of the surrounding architecture. Invisibility is optional: VIPs can make themselves appear, like elevated divinities, to the dancers below by adjusting the internal lighting of the structures. The interiors are furnished with banquette-cum-beds, encouraging Bacchanalian behaviour.

Avalon's restrooms are more than bog standard. 'The toilets should be as social as anywhere else. Lots goes on in the bathrooms at clubs,' says Sam O'Donahue. Unisex cubes of aluminium-framed honeycomb Panelite, back-lit with fluorescents, are set at oblique angles to the host room, and glow white against the polished, black porcelain-tiled floors. Warm interiors of red and bright yellow invite patrons to step inside these modern light installations.

Desgrippes Gobé's energizing renovation has brought the club beaming into the modern age. From out of the darkness, you could say that Avalon has finally found the light.

below
VIPs are accommodated in
the lofty heights of the Prop
Room, with its own bar.

bottom
Floor-to-ceiling, internally
lit resin rods illuminate the
Reed Room.

crobar / New York, USA

Callin Fortis and Lionel Ohayan, December 2003

crobar is one of a crop of new superclubs that have
been unleashed on New Yorkers over the past
couple of years. Like many of the other venues,
it is located in Manhattan's destination *du soir*,
Chelsea, and is the third crobar to emerge in the
US, with sister clubs in Chicago and Miami, all
owned by Callin Fortis and Ken Smith. crobar
follows in the nightclub tradition of being forged
from a reclaimed industrial warehouse space, and
is apparently the first large-scale venue to be built
from virgin property in New York in over a decade.
A mammoth 2,320 square metres (25,000 square
feet), the club occupies three buildings that,
together, span an entire city block.

Fortis and his Big Time Design studio, in
collaboration with Lionel Ohayan and ICRAVE
Design Studio, were responsible for the interior,
which integrates state-of-the-art technology with
the existing fabric and character of the warehouse,
and, in its use of such materials as copper and
steel, retains its early twentieth-century metal-
foundry legacy. He likens 'the sociology of
nightclub design' to creating a roller-coaster ride,
and uses the analogy of the Roman Coliseum
when describing his approach. 'The people's
experience of the "event" and view of the
gladiators varied from man to man, based
solely on the designer's ability to manipulate
flow through space,' he explains. He goes on to
say, 'I ask hundreds of tactical questions. I want
to encourage emotion and disassociative
experience' (*Loft*, April 2004).

Major structural renovations, including the
addition of new floors and staircases, were carried
out to create a venue with three interconnecting
spaces: the Main Room, Reed Room and Prop
Room (for VIPs). 'crobar's voyeuristic personality
derives from architect Steven Holl's theory of
three connections of space. Each space can be
approached from multiple vantage points, none
of which ever reveals the whole,' explains Fortis.

The throbbing heart of the venue is the vast
Main Room, measuring 930 square metres (10,000
square feet), which accommodates 1,500 clubbers
in a space devoted to dancing, although there is
also a large, asymmetric trapezoid-shaped bar,
featuring a counter top of brass shavings encased
in yellow resin. Taking advantage of the 18 metre
(60 foot) high bow-truss ceiling, Fortis created
a central, 230 square metre (2,500 square foot)

below
The tunnel connecting the
Main Room to the Reed Room.

dance floor and framed it with 'soaring, sculptural demi-arches'. These support a wrap-around mezzanine (allowing for arena-style voyeurism), which encircles a 30 x 10 metre (100 x 32 foot) video-projection media wall and 'floating', copper-clad DJ booth, that juts out over the heads of dancing patrons.

Cutting-edge technology is in full effect – while reigning from on high, the DJ can flash messages to the crowd by programming a 'LED ticker', installed beneath the elevated booth. Lighting effects include light pods that rise and fall, and dynamic laser beams that zip around the room. Whether the entire room is suddenly bleached white with light, or freezing-cold nitrogen clouds descend from above, to cool the clubbers below, it is technology that provides the drama.

The Main Room is connected to the Reed Room by a 3.5 metre (12 foot) wide by 3 metre (10 foot) long tunnel, referred to by Fortis as a threshold. 'Once inside, there is literally NO TURNING BACK. That makes the heart beat faster, the palms sweat, and adrenaline pump. Inside, I installed "white noise" generators that cancel the two disparate sound frequencies of the other rooms and create a moment of silence once you step inside,' says Fortis. 'That's a bit of humour in a nightclub that is "all about music". As you exit the tunnel, the hairs on the back of your neck stand up. You can't help but want to dance and smile' (*Loft*, April 2004).

Towering, illuminated resin rods provide yellow shafts of light in the Reed Room, at juxtaposition with the midnight-blue light that emanates from the open-grate ceiling. Raw, durable surfaces abound in this 250-capacity space; exposed warehouse brick and a concrete bar are upstaged by an intriguing backdrop of chain-mail curtain, revealing the secrets of the ladies' room beyond.

Luxury is reserved for VIPs in the barrel-shaped Prop Room, described as '60s-ski-lodge-meets-Barbarella'. Original wood beams have been retained in this loft-like space, which is lent a golden hue by the burnished copper leaf of the domed ceiling. A series of niches in the walls, illuminated in different colours, animate the room. The timber bar, with lighting recessed below the counter top, casts a warm glow in the midst of the space. Finishes are luxurious, with perimeter banquettes of tan mock-crocodile and black marble tables, making this a cosy haven providing respite from the hedonistic chaos of the Main Room.

Kabaret's Prophecy / London, UK

David Collins, April 2004

Twenty-first-century clubland is rainbow bright. Revolutionary technologies are producing spectacular lighting, which is rejuvenating nocturnal spaces. Kabaret's Prophecy is one of the most dazzling examples of this. The 100-capacity interior is an electro-glitterbox of LEDs, which flash and change colour in time with the music.

Located in London's Soho, this 'boutique' club is a collaborative effort, with David Collins at the helm. Best known for his luxurious restaurant projects, Collins was determined to produce something new and exciting for his first nightclub commission. 'I wanted to integrate sound and light, but didn't want to rely on the predictable clichés of glitterball or flashing ceiling lights. It had to be a more sophisticated, avant-garde solution.'

Collins asked hologram and laser-light wizard Chris Levine to work with him, and he also brought environmental-graphics engineers and live-performance video specialists UVA (United Visual Artists) on board. 'Together, we decided the interior should feature a constantly evolving light show,'

says Collins, 'created using the latest LED and computer programming to make it vibrant and responsive to the mood of the room and the music.' UVA, in turn, teamed up with video-system experts Creative Technology to develop a bespoke installation for the venue. UVA adapted their advanced visual technology and software that they had designed and developed for Massive Attack's '100th Window' and Basement Jaxx's 'Kish Kash' live tours in 2003/2004. Two adjacent walls in the club feature a single kinetic-image backdrop, constructed from modular, intelligent-LED pixel blocks (MiPIX by Barco), upon which graphics, 3-D images and video content, rendered by a real-time graphics engine and triggered by a MIDI keyboarder, appear, producing an ever-changing visual environment.

above
VJs mix visuals for the walls from the
DJ booth, with many different colours
and formations possible.

right
Verner Panton globe lights hang above
the Swarovksi crystal-studded bar,
which is lit by ultra-violet LEDs to
make it sparkle.

opposite
Kabaret's Prophecy's dazzling LED
canvas measures 17.8 x 1.2 metres
(58 x 4 feet).

Kabaret's Prophecy is an ongoing project. Creative Technology are responsible for the supply and integration of the MiPIX wall and UVA for the continued art direction of the screen content and personnel controlling the GFX. UVA's resident video jockeys (aka the VJs) control and mix the visuals live each night from a computer with a musical-instrument-style MIDI keyboard, manipulating the blinking canvas of 3,000 LEDs to alter the ambience. The possible lighting permutations are vast, from graduated waves, patterns and textured effects, through repeated bitmap images, to starry explosions – all locked into the beat of the music.

Levine installed lasers at the top of the central support column, which shoot red beams out across the ceiling above the dance floor. Reflecting the maximalism of the kaleidoscopic walls is the jewel-encrusted bar. Its smoked-grey mirror façade is studded with 3,000 Swarovski crystals, delicately back-lit with ultra-violet and regular LED light to cast coloured shadows onto the surrounding reflective surfaces.

Collins deliberately chose a monochromatic colour scheme to optimize the lighting effects throughout the interior. Semi-circular booths are upholstered in soft, graphite leather, with tiny perforations that echo the flamboyant, swirling motif of the bar façade. Table tops, bearing a fine dot-matrix pattern and laminated with mirror, replicate and reflect the wall display.

Dancing in Kabaret's Prophecy is like starring in an ever-evolving pop video. Such techno-bling effects are bound to seduce any clubber.

right
Seating booths are upholstered in leather, bearing the same swirling motif as the crystal-studded bar.

Sonotheque / Chicago, USA

Suhail Design Studio, December 2002

Donnie Madia, the man behind Chicago's sleek, minimalist Blackbird restaurant, teamed up with fellow restaurateur Terry Alexander and local DJ Joe Bryl to hatch Sonotheque. The shared ambition of this 'trio of Chicago's nightlife style-makers' was to create a nocturnal environment dedicated to music, 'designed first as an acoustically precise room for a world-class sound system and second as an intimate lounge'.

Suhail, designer of various Chicago hotspots (such as cocktail/dessert bar Sugar) and of the house set for MTV's *Real World*, was enlisted to realize their dreams. In his quest for sonic perfection, Suhail adapted existing acoustical materials, and used them throughout the project, from the discreet façade to the pared-down interior. 'I wanted the design to be dictated by music. I wanted sound to be the colour,' says the local designer. Hence the reduced, monochromatic aesthetic of the 325 square metre (3,500 square foot) venue, located in the increasingly gentrified West Side neighbourhood.

Sonotheque's understated, but distinctive, street presence consists of a grey aluminium cladding and features a vertical strip of custom-designed, aluminium-powder-coated geometric tiles, set at various angles. Its anonymity is intentional; as Suhail explains, 'I wanted people to know that something is there. But only people who need to know will figure it out.' The exterior tiles are used on the interior's ceiling also, providing a certain visual continuity, thus guiding patrons into the space. They also serve to diffuse sound evenly through the venue.

The rectilinear interior is organized simply, with, on one side, a bar and a slightly raised seating area, enveloped by a dark, timber-effect vinyl floor and ceiling. Every element was carefully considered in acoustic terms. White ceiling tiles, cut into narrow strips, are stacked like bricks along the wall above the bar, reinforcing the clean horizontality of the space. Bespoke bar stools, upholstered in dove-grey Ultra Suede, line the bar, which features a durable Zodiaq-quartz bar top, manufactured by DuPont.

above
The anonymous aluminium-clad exterior with its strip of geometric tiles.

opposite
Most of the décor – from the ceiling to the wall panels – enhances acoustics.

Low-slung, modular seating runs along the perimeter of the elevated lounge area. Manufactured from high-density foam and, again, Ultra Suede, it is designed to reflect high-frequency sound. Industrial sound-boarding and Soundwave's sculptural Snowcrash acoustical panelling serve as the only ornamentation along the walls surrounding the lounge.

Since Sonotheque is all about the music, the DJ takes centre stage, housed in an elevated luminous booth, made of floor-to-ceiling sand-blasted glass panels, with a clear strip for the DJ to see out of. Funktion One speakers, recessed and framed in neon-blue light, form an integral part of the interior and are positioned 'to maximize performance without compromising design'. Suhail's audio-enhancing Sonotheque ensures the walls are alive with the sound of jazz-based music.

right
The minimalist bar features custom-made stools and a durable Zodiaq-quartz top, made by DuPont.

below
Snowcrash acoustical panelling provides the only adornment in the lounge area.

above
A screen of vertical metal bars separates the dance floor from the bar area.

right
The grid of lights is computer-programmed to synchronize and change colour with the beat of the music.

Tripping the light fantastic has gone disco crazy. Designers across the globe are rekindling the halcyon days of *Saturday Night Fever* through the futuristic application of LEDs, fibre optics and neon lighting. When Brazilian designer Muti Randolph was approached by DJ Renato Ratier to create an 'impressive and unique environment, with good acoustics that would please a diverse clubbing crowd', he, too, decided that the lighting would be the key architectural element.

The sequel to the D-Edge in Campo Grande, the São Paulo venue features a grid of perspex and metal boxes, containing RGB neon bulbs, in an all-black 600-capacity interior. 'I chose black for all the "material" elements in order to make them disappear, letting the virtual, dynamic light architecture prevail,' says Randolph. 'In the dance area, the light strips are sunken into a concrete floor (which is coated in black resin) and into the black-painted timber walls. Above, they are suspended from the ceiling.'

Randolph describes his blinking lightbox as a 3-D matrix. 'The interior is like a computer monitor, but, instead of pixels, lines of light are programmed by a computer to radiate various colours (generated by combinations of red, green and blue) and flash to the beat,' he explains. 'My goal was to make people actually see the music, to give rhythm

to space and colour to sound.' Behind the DJ booth and small, adjoining VIP lounge, three giant LED audio-spectrum analyzers, connected to the music system, rise and fall like colossal graphic equalizers, animating the wall and enhancing the visual materialization of the music.

A screen of vertical, square metal bars divides the dance floor from the bar and lounge. To aid socializing and relaxation, Randolph has reduced the light presence here to a minimum. Four seating booths are defined by a series of parallel lines from floor to ceiling. Each booth is furnished with black-vinyl upholstered banquettes, accompanied by simple, black wooden tables and benches. The bar counter is constructed from black-lacquered wood and displays a façade with apparently receding vertical stripes, echoing the luminous Cartesian geometry that frames D-Edge.

above
View of the bar area shows seating booths and the bar opposite.

Zouk / Kuala Lumpur, Malaysia

ZDR Studio, March 2004

The arrival of superclub Zouk awards Kuala Lumpur's serious status in the global clubbing stakes. The Malaysian capital has been on the hedonist's party circuit for a while, but Zouk gives the city real cachet. Built on an acre of land, the iconic 3,000 square metre (32,000 square foot) bar and club complex takes the brand, which originated in Singapore, to an exciting new level. Located in the 'Golden Triangle' – an area full of clubs, restaurants and hotels – and within walking distance of the incredible Petronas twin towers, the two-storey structure can accommodate up to 2,000 nocturnal revellers.

The client requested 'something Mediterranean, similar to Zouk Singapore, but also organic freeform, sculptural-like and modern, with an emphasis on building as form and icon with references to Hassan Fathy and Philippe Starck'. Starck requires little introduction and appears elsewhere in this book. Fathy, however, was an important Egyptian architect (1899–1989), who believed in responsible architecture. He promoted the notion that traditional and vernacular architecture, using natural resources, should be valued and respected. Fathy often adopted classic Arab elements in his work, in particular adobe, and adapted them for the twenty-first century.

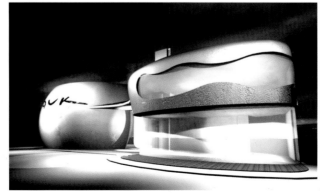

left
Computer renderings show different views of Zouk's twin blobs.

far left
The distinctive exterior, complete with outdoor seating area, by night.

Zouk's bulbous exterior echoes amoebic forms. It should be read in the context of recent trends in 'blobular', or biomorphic, architecture. The façade, animated by signage and curvilinear, glazed apertures, manages to be futuristic without appearing starkly alien. Beneath the whitewashed stucco exterior is a steel skeleton, with wire mesh creating the curvaceous shape, with a top layer of traditional bricks.

A central entrance, flanked by the two blobs, opens into a double-height tunnel, which forks. The left branch leads to the main Zouk Club, housed in the whitewashed form, and host to international and resident dance-music DJs. The right-hand passage leads to a glazed wing, containing the more intimate Velvet Underground, Loft Bar (named after David Mancuso's legendary disco parties) and Terrace Bar.

Inside the venue, Fathy's influence becomes abundantly clear. ZDR have combined natural materials with synthetics to achieve organic surfaces and textures. An ochre adobe wall lends warmth to the cloakroom arrival area. Beyond, the meandering alley and cement-plaster interior of the double-height main-club area appear carved out from underground rock.

above
The main club, with surrounding mezzanine and bar, and DJ booth below.

right
Cracked mosaic finishes on this seating niche display the organic influences on the project's design.

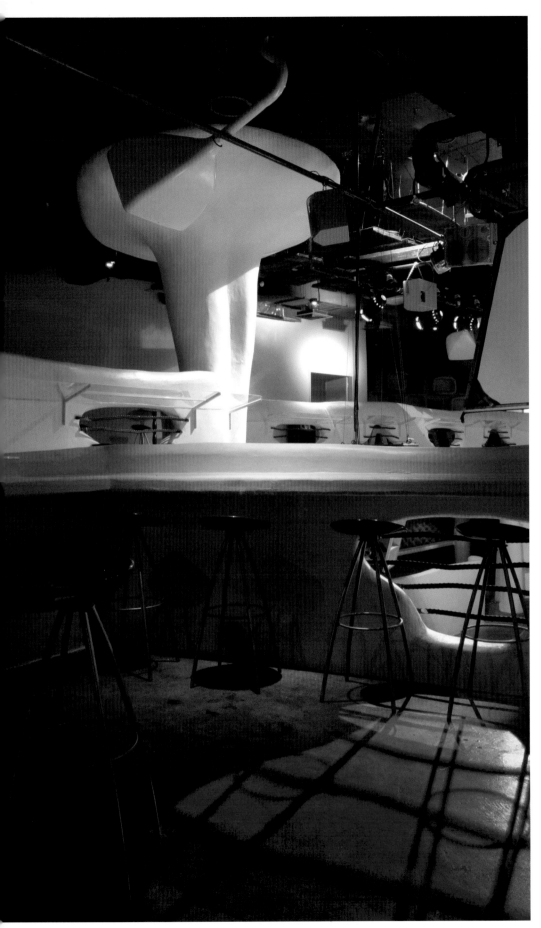

left
View of the mezzanine
seating area, which overlooks
the dance floor.

The organic plasterwork continues in the design of the bar. Tucked beneath the mezzanine, it glows warmly, with a façade decorated by back-lit fibreglass panels and internally lit niches for bottle displays on the back bar. The central DJ booth is elevated, with a lozenge-shaped aperture allowing commanding views of the sunken (cement-hardened-concrete) dance floor.

In the neighbouring wing, Velvet Underground has a timber-lined dance floor. Walls lined in tessellated triangles of fabric provide texture and help acoustics. A carpeted lounge is furnished with custom-designed, curvilinear furniture in bold elementary hues. The bar is considerably slicker than that in the main Zouk club, with a counter top of magenta Lumigraf, laminated onto glass panels, and a façade of magenta-painted stone in a sawn finish.

In the Wine Terrace, the bar is reminiscent of Herzog & de Meuron's Dominus Winery in California's Napa Valley. Polished, grey river pebbles, contained in stainless-steel netting, are back-lit to emphasize their organic nature. Meanwhile, the back-bar finish is inspired by marine life; Axolotyl-metal plates in varying colours have been arranged to replicate fish scales. Up in the Loft, patrons can recline in club chairs and survey the world outside, softly framed by the biomorphic curves of the window.

below left
One of the bars, constructed from grey river pebbles encased in stainless-steel netting, then back-lit to give a fiery glow.

below right
Hassan Fathy's influences are clear in this adobe wall finish.

opposite
In the Loft Bar, guests can look out of this curvy window on the world.

overleaf left
Bright, elementary coloured furniture animates this lounge space.

overleaf right
A tentlike canopy forms an intimate lounge area.

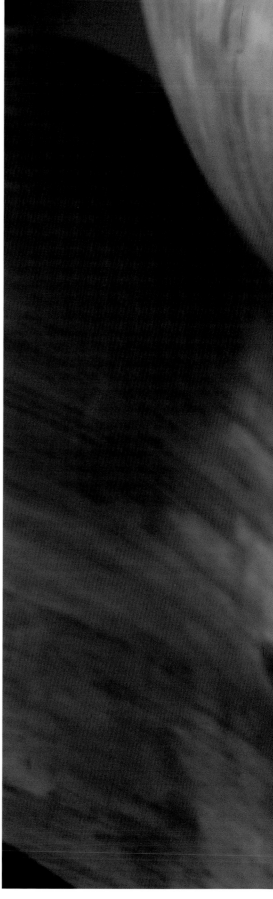

Chapter 4: Clubs

Coconclub / Moscow, Russia

··

Savinkin/Kuzmin, November 2002

Moscow's Coconclub rises up like a giant termite mound. Bulging against the confines of its host building, it echoes, in an earthly, organic way, the silver-cloud forms of Jakob + MacFarlane's Georges restaurant on top of Paris's Pompidou Centre. Architects Vladislav Savinkin and Vladimir Kuzmin describe the project as a 'four-level biomorphic formation, like a mountain peppered with caves, suddenly put inside a building with an eclectic façade'.

Asked to create a VIP restaurant-club, Savinkin/Kuzmin decided to create an extremely different environment to that offered by the existing property, which they characterize as 'An example of post-Soviet, postmodern architecture, with all the archetypal features: symmetrical square plan, arch windows, simplicity of façade, classical details, etc.' Their blond 'chrysalis' departs from these formal limitations, emerging as an independent volume within the main space, 'an amoeba-shaped body with holes and caves, absolutely ignorant to the outer-framed architecture'. The 400 square metre (4,300 square foot) 'body' houses a basement bar, with dance floor and toilets, a bar and restaurant on the ground floor, a first-floor bar, with dance floor and restaurant, and a chill-out zone and toilet on the second floor. These various levels are connected by a transparent glass stairway; suspended from the ceiling, it spirals around the outer skin of the body.

left and opposite
Smooth, sanded surfaces of
the precision-cut plywood
cocoon shown in detail.

right
The 'termite mound' includes
a toilet capsule, accessible via
a small glass walkway.

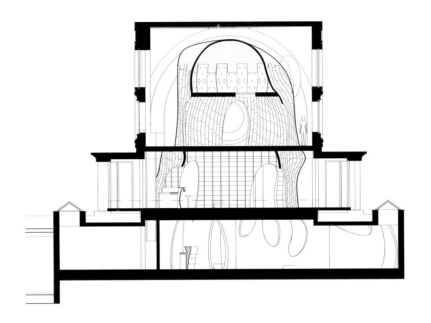

section
The organic mound rises up inside the host building.

left
Apertures cut into the plywood structure allow for natural light.

Chapter 4: Clubs

opposite and left
Transparent glass stairs, suspended from the ceiling, wind up around the cocoon to provide access to the various levels.

above
The organic form creates cosy nooks and niches for guests.

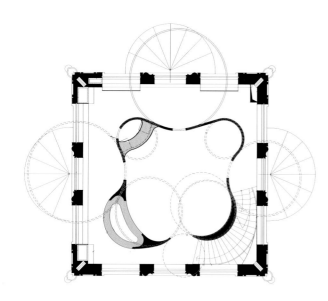

plan
The curvy plywood structure
was created with computer-
aided design using an
arrangement of circles.

above
Coconclub's post-Soviet,
postmodern façade by night.

above
The loft at the top, with
timber and ice-like plastic
stools.

Initially, Savinkin/Kuzmin visualized a 'Russian Gehry', as in a metal construction, but the cost was prohibitive. 'Instead, we decided to build the body slice by slice from precision-cut plywood, a flexible material capable of creating complex forms.' To achieve this, the duo produced two working models: a 3-D computerized model, consisting of simple, circle-based plans, to calculate the exact section, or 'moulds', and an actual 1:10 scale model, constructed from pieces of Foam-X, to finalize the exact shape.

The computer-aided design drawings were multiplied by ten to make templates for the plywood sheets, which were then laid horizontally, one on top of the other, to build the shell. 'The technique consists of carpenters and craftsmen bevelling a mass of plywood sheets at different angles. It really grew like an organic creature, so it was a very natural solution, which is far more home-grown Russian than Gehry!' Hours of sanding and the shine of varnish have produced a slippery smooth, undulating surface, which is evocative of rock that has been eroded by the elements.

Apertures are aligned with the existing windows, flooding the many caves with natural light. Complementing the organic aesthetic, Savinkin/Kuzmin have furnished the venue with Sturm und Plastic's range of transparent plastic seating; Gamine and Bloody Mary chairs and Ondo stools appear as if carved from ice. The chill-out grotto at the top of the structure is the most intimate space, a Gaudiesque attic with its very own satellite pod, accessible via a glass walkway. This 'floating' enclosure, supported by a plywood-clad metal pipe, houses a VIP toilet. Whether patrons emerge as butterflies remains to be seen.

above
Coconclub's distinctive toilet
pod, with its sliding door.

CocoonClub / Frankfurt, Germany

3deluxe, July 2004

CocoonClub is, without doubt, one of the most exciting new clubs of the twenty-first century. The constantly changing, semi-virtual interior raises the stakes in the seemingly endless quest of operators, DJs and designers to produce über-dynamic nocturnal spaces that will keep the notoriously fickle clubbing crowd entertained. Guests are encouraged to leave reality behind as they enter this 'three-dimensional interface', and to lose themselves in a cocktail of music, images and light, which are 'played' acoustically and visually by a DJ and VJ.

Progeny of global DJ-superstar Sven Väth (aka the 'Godfather of Techno'), this pioneering venue promises to revive Frankfurt's reputation as an international clubbing destination and *the* 'playground of the electronic-music avant-garde'. This 'field experiment for transforming space and perception' occupies the ground floor of the distinctive, triangular U.F.O. loft building, a mixed-use property in the Ostend district of the city.

The venue is divided into four areas; at its heart, and echoing the geometry of the host building, is the triangular CocoonClub, incorporating a 570 square metre (6,100 square foot) dance floor. Adjoining this is the InBetween Lounge and two restaurants, ClubRestaurant Micro and BedRestaurant Silk. The 'genetic architecture' of the interior was developed over a two-year period by Wiesbaden-based, interdisciplinary design agency 3deluxe.

A four-strong team designed CocoonClub: Dieter Brell and Nik Schweiger are responsible for the interiors and Andreas and Stephan Lauhoff devised the graphics. Their organic influences are most evident in the club itself, with its landscaped dance floor of curved mini-platforms, with illuminated edges. The space is enclosed by a 'permeable cell membrane' wall, which 3deluxe developed in CAD, then producing a gypsum prototype. The final version is constructed from steel and clad in two layers of perforated Flowstone panelling (Flowstone is a fine, white concrete), thus providing a blank canvas upon which to project lights, graphics and images. A significant feature of CocoonClub, the membrane structure is used as an abstract motif for the corporate identity.

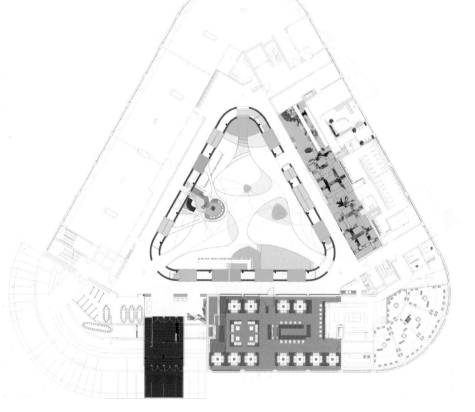

plan
The triangular layout of Cocoon, with the dance floor in the centre.

right
Genetic projections animate one of the vivid-green seating cocoons in the 'membrane wall'.

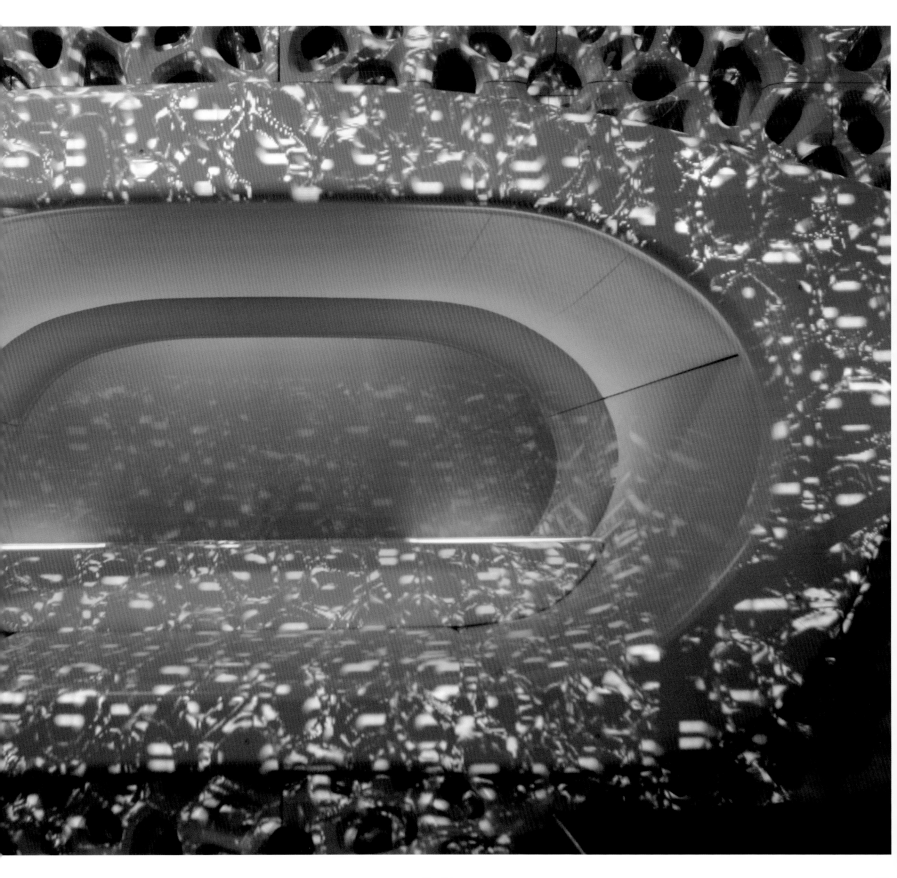

Housed within the membrane wall are 13 capsules, or cocoons, padded in grass-green vinyl and positioned at various heights overlooking the dance-floor action. Some are open and accessible from the dance-floor side of the wall. Others, glazed to offer more privacy, are reached from the calmer areas of the venue, such as the InBetween Lounge.

Three VIP cocoons can be reserved for an evening. Designed as 'modern theatre boxes', they offer reclining occupants a kind of bespoke James-Bond-meets-Space-Odyssey clubbing experience; internal lighting and ventilation are adjustable, and technology enables guests to call the waiter and survey the club goings-on via camera-linked screens.

Appropriately, the most striking feature of the club is the DJ pulpit, which protrudes from the wall like some kind of hovering alien creature or spacecraft, its tentacles stretching out, anchoring it in place. 3deluxe constructed this futuristic altar from steel, clad

above
The DJ rules from the protruding, alien-like pulpit.

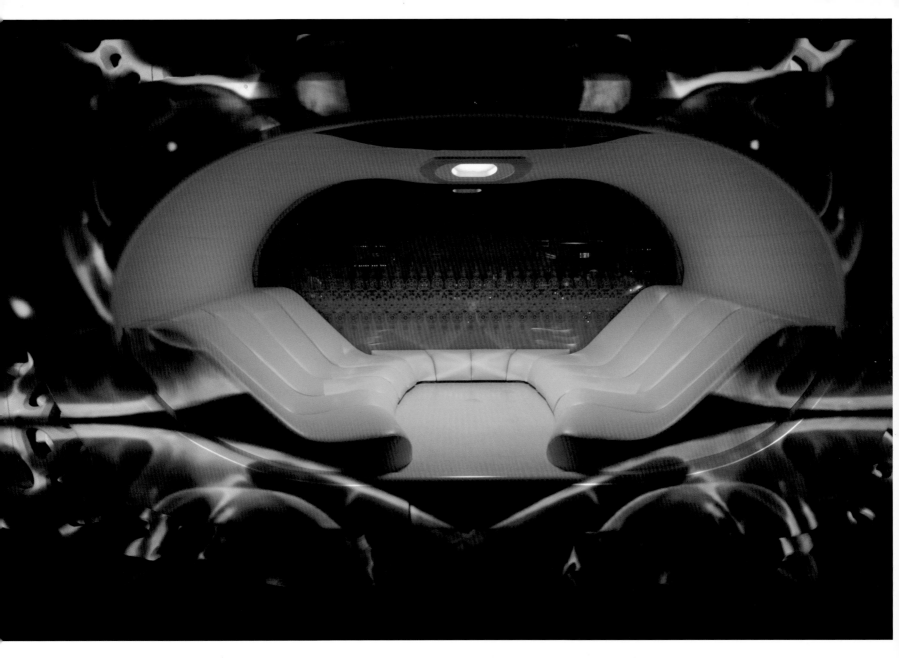

it in hand-routed Styrofoam segments and then sealed it with a smooth, white finish of ceramic fibres. The elevated cockpit affords the DJ and Room Jockey the ideal point from which to dictate the mood and atmosphere of the club.

The visual richness of the CocoonClub continues in the Inbetween Lounge, where the walls burst with giant floral murals, designed by 3deluxe's Andreas and Stephan Lauhoff. A series of large ottomans, illuminated from beneath, lend the floor an eerie glow. Pockets of intimacy are defined by decorative light panels; 'these bluish glass showcases contain a linear grid of cold cathode tubes,' explains Brell. 'Specially programmed software sets the lights aflicker, casting organically shaped shadows across the tube grid.'

above and right
Inhabitants of the seating cocoons can watch the dance-floor action in comfort.

Chapter 4: Clubs

left
The adjoining lounge,
with floral murals, bespoke
ottomans and decorative
lighting panels.

overleaf
ClubRestaurant Micro is
adorned with silver fibre-glass
tubes; suspended from the
ceiling, they create a backdrop
for visual projections.

right
BedRestaurant Silk forms the curved corner section at the top right of this computer rendering.

below
Show storage for guests in the restaurant reception.

ClubRestaurant Micro is an open-plan, multi-functional space, serving Eurasian food from a glazed show kitchen. In the early evening, it operates as a restaurant and lounge, gradually morphing into a club as the night progresses. The dark-timber interior is laid out in a simple grid formation, with a bamboo floor and boxy, cube-shaped furniture, including bamboo-topped tables.

Silver fibreglass tubes of varying lengths, suspended from the ceiling, delineate physically the different areas within ClubRestaurant Micro, without jeopardizing the open-plan atmosphere. Complex multimedia 'ornamentation' is projected onto these vertical elements; these 'aesthetic beamer projections' are synchronized with the music, 'thereby illustrating the various three-dimensional sound spaces, which the DJ produces,' according to Schweiger.

BedRestaurant Silk bears a resemblance to Amsterdam's Supperclub, designed by Concrete. This ethereal, white environment is 'inspired by the Asian and ancient Greco-Roman culinary traditions'. Here, more expensive gourmet food is served, while the design of the space aims to encourage relaxed behaviour.

Guests enter a reception room, where they remove their shoes and put on textile footwear. 'Reclining dining' takes place on eight vast beds, separated by diaphanous gauze screens, and each is capable of accommodating up to nine people. Asian food and drink is served on satin perspex trays, cleverly designed to slot into indentations in the beds' armrests. Recessed lighting is programmed to change colour, bathing the space in various soothing hues. Filigree metal ornaments between the gauze screens provide geometric decoration.

Through a combination of state-of-the-art technology and materials, driven by an incredibly fertile imagination, 3deluxe have created a design tour de force that is destined to thrust twenty-first-century clubbers into the future.

below
Bed areas are separated by transparent gauze screens, and food is served on perspex tray tables.

Quo / New York, USA

Dupoux Design, May 2004

Over the past decade, Manhattan-based 'sculptor of space' Stephane Dupoux
has become the toast of Miami and New York nightlife. First, he seduced the
jet-set crowd in Miami with restaurant-lounge club concepts Pearl and Nikki
Beach. More recently, following the success of New York 'boutique nightclub'
Cielo, his consultancy, Dupoux Design, was asked to create a second
Manhattan club.

Guy Malhotra and Carlo Seneca commissioned the French-born designer
to develop a scheme for a 750 square metre (8,000 square foot) nocturnal
space in West Chelsea. 'One of them loved the work I did in South Beach,
Miami, and wanted something exotic,' says Dupoux, 'and the other wanted
something very New York, so I came up with the concept of Urban
Tropicalism.' The result is the rainbow-bright Quo.

Distinctly Dupoux, Quo is a blend of ergonomic curves, organic materials and forms, with lighting playing a starring role. Despite residing in New York, Dupoux, who spent his childhood on the beaches of the South of France and his early twenties as a ski instructor in the Swiss Alps, remains enthralled by the great outdoors. 'I find inspiration in the association of forms, colours and textures found in nature,' he explains.

The Urban Tropicalism theme, represented by cobblestone wall finishes and perspex bars containing poured sand, is enhanced by a $150,000 lighting system, developed with entertainment-lighting experts Robert Singer Lighting. 'It's utterly bespoke,' says Kale Lucroux from the lighting company of the Color Kinetics LED system. 'It means the club will never have a stagnant feel. You can even project images that create the sense of being under water.'

An astounding 16.7 million different colours are achievable in the space. Multi-hued water columns and audio-linked wall panels change colour, image and intensity in time with the music. LEDs are programmed to produce the effect of water trickling down the stone wall. Dupoux-designed chandeliers, constructed from 15 centimetre (6 inch) white perspex tubes, containing LEDs inserted inside circular or square pieces of wood to diffuse the light, are the main source of illumination.

At the heart of the space is the curved bar, crowned by a lighting panel that follows the arching sweep of the back wall. Designed to complement the lighting fixtures, it comprises 25 1.8 metre (6 foot) perspex tubes, housing 1.5 metre (5 foot) LEDs, mounted to the wall by horizontal timber arcs. Robert Singer Lighting programmed the panel to radiate either single colours, a 'chasing rainbow effect', or to flash, disco-style. With its dramatic, technologically advanced light creations, Quo is anything but the status quo.

above left
The DJ reigns from a vinyl-upholstered, cup-shaped booth (to the right of picture).

left
The state-of-the-art lighting system includes internally lit, water-filled perspex columns, which glow ever-changing rainbow shades.

Powder / New York, USA

Karim Rashid, November 2002

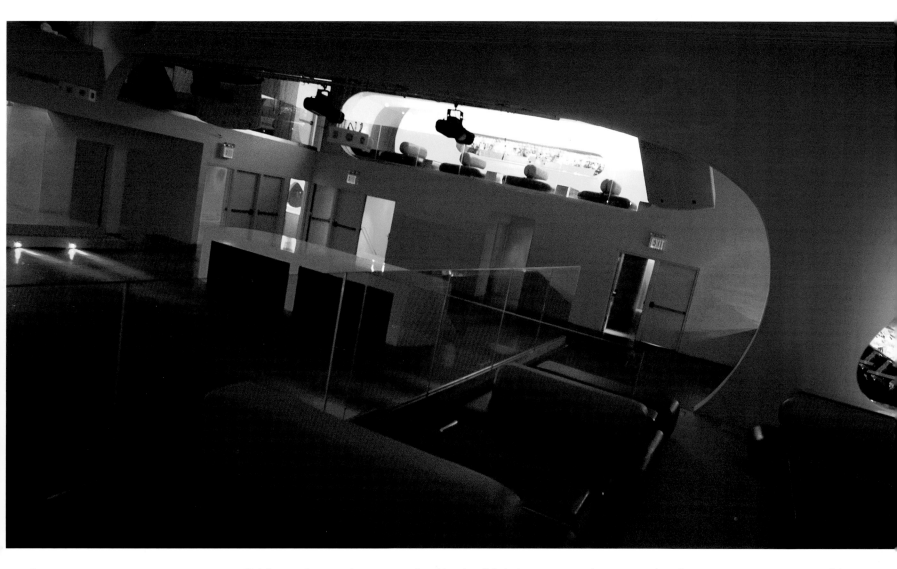

above
Raised seating areas overlook the dancefloor, separated by balustrades of orange laminated glass.

opposite left
Visitors ascend a pink, glowing entrance staircase.

plans, opposite right
From bottom, plans of the main level and mezzanine.
1. safe area, 2. bar, 3. grazing bar, 4. stage, 5. dance floor, 6. seating, 7. mezzanine, 8. DJ lounge, 9. DJ

Rainbow colours and curves overlap, blend and fade in the amorphous cloud that is Powder, the Karim Rashid-designed club located in New York's Meatpacking District. The Cairo-born, US-based designer is best known for his candy-coloured products and bare-faced declarations on design; his monograph, published in 2002, was entitled *I Want to Change the World*. In 2004, at a Design Hotels forum, Rashid said he believed everything to be industrial design, 'because everything is now manifested around technology and almost robotic production, and, in a sense, architecture has become a kind of composite technique of industrial design.'

It's no wonder then that Rashid has progressed to designing entire interiors, such as the award-winning Morimoto restaurant in Philadelphia (as featured in *Restaurant Design*) and the Semiramis Hotel in Athens. Powder exemplifies his studio's preoccupation with playing with perceptions of space. 'In the material

environment today, there are so many new materials and affordances that can allow us to project the space infinitely. We take pieces of glass, films, all kinds of layering and light and are perpetually trying to find a way to create immaterial space.'

Powder no longer operates as a nightclub. However, it does function as an events space, and rumour has it that it may re-open. As with many dramatic venues, the anonymous, grey stucco façade belies the exciting, multi-coloured pop interior. Entering via translucent pink-glass doors, guests are immediately immersed in a hot-pink wonderland. Epoxy floors and walls have been painted in the colour, and each tread of the glowing staircase that ascends to the club is illuminated by a beam of light shone through pink gel to accentuate the hue.

The 1,200 square metre (12,900 square foot) interior comprises a 900 square metre (9,700 square foot) main space and 300 square metre (3,200 square foot)

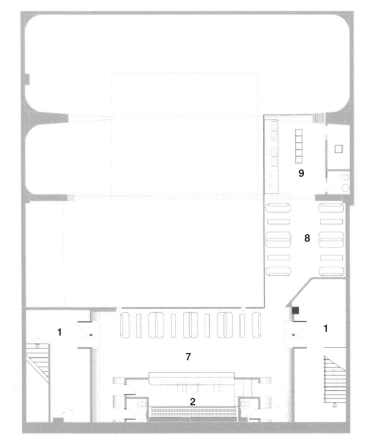

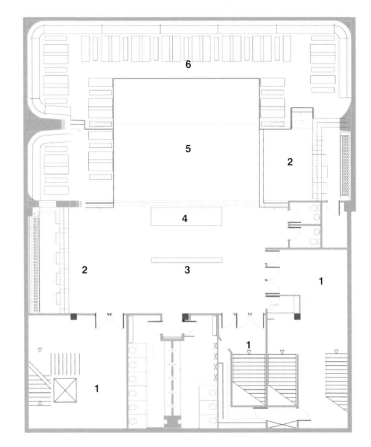

above
Recessed lighting in the
ceiling casts a warm glow
over the bar area.

above
Amoeba-shaped apertures
and curved walls are the
designer's self-described
'birthmark'.

above
The lime-green mezzanine
enclosure offers a rose-tinted
view of the club below.

above

The prevailing colours are continued in the custom-designed, purple and orange vinyl seating.

mezzanine, with only translucent coloured-glass partitions dividing areas. Rashid's signature curvilinear and radius forms dominate, from the 'amoeba-shaped' aperture that frames the recessed cashier kiosk, and the curved walls and many 'amorphous cuts', described by the designer as 'birthmarks', made throughout the internal structure, to the bespoke furniture.

On the ground floor, raised seating areas overlook a centrally positioned, purple epoxy-coated dance floor, bordered by balustrades of orange laminated glass. Specially designed furniture continues the colour combo, with low, lozenge-like benches of purple and orange vinyl. Chartreuse glass tables echo the horizontal curves of the seating. The mezzanine level is brighter, with lime-green floors, walls and ceiling merging to form a capsule-like enclosure. Rose-tinted views of the club below are possible through the pink laminated-glass balustrade.

Bars are a glowing enticement for guests. Their façades have been clad in dichromatic glass, which reflects various colours. Digitally programmed LED lighting is recessed behind perimeter banquettes, drenching this environment of infinity walls, translucent boundaries, and fruit-hued surfaces and objects in 140 different and changing shades. Pale-lilac walls soak up the colours well and were chosen specifically for that reason. 'Most dance clubs are really dark,' says Rashid (*Frame*, Issue 32, May/June 2003). 'I was trying to prove that we could take a light space and, using only lighting, get it really dark. I wanted to make a club that would feel airy and breathable, not a place that feels as if you're there to pick up somebody you can't see.'

Project credits

190east
Hanauer Landstr 190
Frankfurt
Germany
www.190east.de
Architecture and Design: Mack + Co.
Architektur und Gestaltung
Lange Strasse 31
60311 Frankfurt
Germany
www.mack-co.de
Project Team: Kay Mack, Christian Damm,
Melanie Gantert
Client: 190east GbR.
Main Contractors:
Carpentry and Finishings: Proforma
Paintings and Mural Paintings: Hartmut
Scholz
Floor: Rockies
Engineering Consultants: Planungsbüro
Röhrig

747 Bar and Lounge
via Roma 112/114
96100 Syracuse
Sicily
Italy
Design and Architecture: L.A. Design
(Leonardo Annecca Architect)
53 rue Montreuil
75011 Paris
France
www.l-a-design.com
Client: Dambaloo srl
Contractors: UNIT
Special Lighting Suppliers: Viabizzuno

L'Angelo Lounge Bar and Dionisio Wine Bar, Aleph Hotel
Via San Basilio 15
Rome
Italy
www.aleph.boscolohotels.com
Design: Tihany Design
135 West 27th Street, 9th Floor
New York, NY 10001
USA
www.tihanydesign.com
Project Team: Adam D. Tihany (Principal
Designer), Rafael Alvarez (Senior Designer),
Peter K. Lu (Project Designer), Andréa
Riecken (Senior Project Designer and
Manager)
Client: Boscolo Group
General Contractor: Giovanni Monzio
Compagnoni srl
MEP Engineer: Intertecno Ingegneria e
Project Management
Audio/Visual Consultant: Tecno Service
Verdari srl
Millwork and Case Goods: Giovanni Monzio
Compagnoni srl
Decorative Lighting: Zonca spa

Decorative Metal: Flava srl
Stone and Tile: Bresciana Graniti spa
Decorative Glass: Venini
Soft Seating and Upholstered Furniture:
Colber srl
Carpet: Motta Moquettes
Window Treatment: Intertende
Art Director: Cristina Beccaria
Elevator artwork: Tazio Secchiaroli Photo
Archive
Artwork in Wine Bar and Restaurant: Nir
Adar

Andy Wahloo
69 rue des Gravilliers
75003 Paris
France
Interior Design and Concept: Hassan Hajjaj
95 Parkway
Camden
London
NW1 7PP
UK
hassan@rapl.demon.co.uk
Architecture: Bruno Caron
Client: Mourad and Hakim Mazouz (MOMO)

Ashibina
3cs Bldg
4F Shinbashi
2-8-9 Minato-ku
Tokyo 105-0004
Japan
http://3cs.co.jp/restaurant/index.html
Interior Design: Zokei Syudan Co. Ltd.
Itou Bldg. 2F 1-8-3 Ebisu Shibuya-ku,
Tokyo 150-1134
Japan
www.zokei-syudan.co.jp
Client: 3CS Hotel & Restaurant Inc.
Contractor: Shiba Sangyou

Avalon
47 West 20th St
(entrance on 6th Avenue)
New York, NY 10011
USA
www.nyavalon.com
Architecture, Interiors and Furniture:
Desgrippes Gobé Group
411 Lafayette St.
New York, NY 10003
USA
www.dga.com
Project Team: Sam O'Donahue, Ayelet
Gezow, Christopher Diereg, David Ashen
Client: Flatiron Entertainment LLC
General Contractor: David Marvisi
Lighting Design: Design 1

Cielo
19 Little West 12th Street
New York, NY 10014
USA
www.cieloclub.com
Interior Design: Dupoux Design
9 East 19th Street
7th Floor
New York, NY 10003
USA
www.dupouxdesign.com
Client: Nicolas Matar & Phillip Reiser
General Contractor: DOA
Finishes/Furniture: Fernando Vara, Evolocity
Inc.
Audio: Dan Agne, Sound Investments
Lighting: Dupoux Design

Coconclub
Prospect Mira, 26, Bldg 7
Moscow
Russia
Closed following a fire at time of going
to press
Interior Architect: Savinkin/Kuzmin Project
Group
Spiridonovka 30/1
Moscow 103001
Russia
v.kuzmin@poledesign.ru
Project Team: Vladimir Kuzmin, Vladislav
Savinkin, Tatiana Tcheliapina, Dmitri
Khromov, Anna Logacheva, Anna
Novoselskaja, Eugenia Tikhonova
Client: Coconclub Moscow
General Contractors: Alfa-Station
(construction and plywood works);
Bioinjector (glass, metal and concrete
works)
Engineer: Bioinjector
Manufacturers: Flat (furniture, fixtures and
fittings)
Plywood: Trend
Lighting: iGuzzini

CocoonClub
Nordendstr 30b
60318 Frankfurt
Germany
www.cocoonclub.net
Interior Design: 3deluxe Interior and Graphic
Design
Schwalbacher Strasse 74
D-65183 Wiesbaden
Germany
www.3deluxe.de
Client: CocoonClub GmbH & Co KG
Show Lighting: Lightpower GmbH
Special Lighting: Karlen-Laber für
Kinetisches Licht
Software, A/V Programming: Meso-Digital
Mdia Systems Design
Gardware and Video Technology: Scrren.NT

Media Consulting: Medienprojekt p2
Installation: Teamtec Media Technology
Sound Design and Technology: Steve
Dash/Phazonsound
Cocoons, DJ Pulpit: Gecco Scene
Construction
InBetweenLounge and Silk Furnishings:
Kessler
Glass work and Light Objects: Glas
Schröder
Metalwork: Steel Work
Flowstone Panels and Membrane Wall: Villa
Rocca
Steel Construction in Membrane Wall and
DL Pulpit: Bürklin
Pneumatic Wall: biggAir
Furnishings at Micro: Klunder
Acrylic glass at Silk: Polymehr
Fabrics and Silk: Eickelmann
Aluminium Ornaments at Silk: Reborn

crobar
Correspondence c/o
crobar/Director of Public Relations
530 West 28th Street
New York, NY 10001
USA
jkrauss@crobar.com
www.crobar.com
Interior Design: Big Time Design, ICRAVE
Design Studio
Architect: Telesco Associates
Project Team – Design: Callin Fortis, Lionel
Ohayan, Siobhan Barry, Orlando Lamas,
Shawn Hope, Tonya Rife
Project Team – Architecture: Callin Fortis,
Tom Telesco, Orlando Lamas
Client: crobar, New York
General Contractor: Bond and Walsh
Project Management: East End Builders
Group
Project Manager: Jonathan Rubin
Project Team – Construction: Carmen
Cuomo, Ed Hogan
HVAC: Asoria Mechanical
Electric: Follender Electric
Plans/Expediter: RIP Associates
Sound: Phazon Sound, Steve Dash
Architectural Lighting: Focus Lighting
AV/DNA Wall: Art Fag
Video: Vello Vierkouse
Specialty Fabrication: Formed concrete bar:
Gregory Turner/Haag Construction
Specialty Graphics: Applied Images
Floor: Ardex by Flooring Solutions
Reed Room Tables: Shaw/Young Metal
Design
Seating: DUNE, Munrod Upholstery
Chainmail drapery: Cascade Coil
Fin-wall cladding: FormGlas Canada
Resin Reeds: Fiberglass World
Prop Room Ceiling: Copper Leafing by
Evergreen, Steve Blum decorating

Perforated Metal Sink: Perfect Circle
Artistic metal work & metal sink:
Shaw/Young Metal Design
Main Bar Material: 'Alkemi' by Renewed
Materials LLC
Custom Tile: Hunnell Street Tile Works
Metallic Tile: Nemo Tile
Subway Tile: Nemo Tile
Pedal Faucets: Chicago Faucets
Recycled 'stone' at cashier wall: Coverings
etc.
Bathroom partitions: Lumasite
Finish Millwork: Millwork Plus
Privalite Glass Wall/VIP Room: Elmont Glass
Privalite Columns: Form Glass
Glass panels: Klahr Glass
Distressed steel: Metal Works, Inc.
Metal DJ Booth & Exterior Awning, Tunnel
Tile Floor:
Gregory Turner/Haag Construction

Crystal
243 Monot Street
Achrafieh
Bierut
Lebanon
www.circlemg.com
Design: Gatserelia Design
Sodeco Square
Bloc D 10th Floor
Beirut
Lebanon
www.gatsereliadesign.com
Project Team: Gregory Gatserelia (Head
Designer), Sinaïda Challita
Client: Crystal Five Co. SARL
Main Contractor: Sites Design & Build
Site Architect: Jimmy Zammar
Steelwork: Feghali Steels
Lighting: Lumière Group
Woodwork: Frem Wood
False Ceiling: Fahim Khoury Co.
Artistic Painting: Brigitte Van Laethum
Fabric: Wardé

D-Edge
Almeda Olga 170
Barra Funda
São Paulo
Brazil
www.d-edge.com.br
Architect: Muti Randolph
Praia de Botafogo, 68/601
22250-040 Rio de Janeiro RJ
Brazil
www.muti.cx
Project Team: Muti Randolph, Carol Bueno,
Paulo Filisetti
Client: Renato Ratier
General Contractor: Triptyque
Lighting Manufacturers: New Light (neon),
ICB (LED's equalizer), Lunardi (dmx)
Wood Furniture: Silvestre de Oliveira

Wall Cushion: Claudio Alves
Glasses: Geraldo Cruz
Mason: Gilberto dos Santos
Poliuretanic Resin: Adraina Addam

Hotel Derlon Bar
Onze Lieve Vrouweplein 6
6211 HD Maastricht
The Netherlands
www.derlon.nl
Interior Design: SEVV
Nieuwpoortkade 2a
1055 RX Amsterdam
The Netherlands
www.sevv.com
Client: Paul Rinkens, Hotel La Bergere
Main Contractor: Arn Meijs Architects

Divina Disco
Via Crocefisso 27
Milan 201231
Italy
Interior Design: Fabio Novembre
Via Mecenate 76/3
Milan
Italy
www.novembre.it
Project Team: Fabio Novembre, Lorenzo De
Nicola, Carlo Formisano
Client: Bunko srl
Contractor: Tecnobeton
Floor-covering: Opus glass mosaic, Bisazza;
Gres ceramic, Keope
Wall-covering: Gemme glass mosaic,
Bisazza
Ceilings: Cumputerized glass mosaic,
Bisazza
Special Structures: Digital prints on Trevira
by Extralarge srl
Lighting: RGB neon system by Light Video
Sound snc
Furniture: Almo srl

Drop Kick
1F, 5-2-14 Roppongi
Minato-ku
Tokyo
Japan
Interior Design: Glamorous Co. Ltd.
1F, 7-6 Omasu-cho, Ashiya
659-0066 Hyogo
Japan
www.glamorous.co.jp
Project Team: Yasumichi Morita, Akihiro Fujii
Client: Naoki Ito
General Contractor: Miysui Designtec Co.
Ltd.
Lighting Consultant: Takashi Harada (Daiko
Electric Co. Ltd.)
Furniture: Complex (Lef Inc)
Graphic Designer: Shoei Ito

Hajime
B1F Iraka Ginza
6-4-7 Ginza
Chuo-ku
Tokyo
Japan
www.ginza-hajime.com
Interior Design: Glamorous Co. Ltd.
Address as above
Project Team: Yasumichi Morita, Daisuke
Watanabe
Client: Nichiei Kogyo Co. Ltd. (President –
Kazuya Nambu)
Contractor: Tansei TDC Co. Ltd.
Lighting Consultant: Kenji Ito (Maxray Inc.)
Graphic Design: Cozmo

Helsinki Club
Yliopistonkatu 8
00100 Helsinki
Finland
www.helsinkiclub.com
Concept and Interior Design: M41LH2
Kalliolanrinne 4A8
00510 Helsinki
Finland
www.M41LH2.com
Project Team: Johanna Hyrkäs, Tommi
Mäkynen, Tuomas Toivonen, Tuomas
Siitonen
Client: Sokotel Oy
Collaborators: Anteeksi (design); Kevan
Shaw Lighting Design (lighting)

Hi Hotel France
3 avenue des Fleurs
0600 Nice
France
www.hi-hotel.net
Concept and Interior Design: matali crasset
productions
26 rue du Buisson Saint-Louis
75010 Paris
France
www.matalicrasset.com
Concept: matali crasset in collaboration with
Philippe Chapalet and Patrick Elouardghi
Interior Design, Decoration and Graphic Art:
matali crasset with the assistance of
Christophe Thelisson, Iscar Diaz and Francis
Fichot
Executive Architect: Frédéric Ducic
Client: Hi Hotel, Joerg Boehler
General Contractor: Philippe Chapelet,
Patrick Elouardghi, HCF sarl.
Concrete Construction: Jean-Marc Lasry,
Lasry & Moro Engineers
Glass: Miroiterie Niçoise, Glasstini
Furniture: Modular
Furniture/Woodwork: Demichelis, Atelier de
la Reinière, Atelier Virginie Ecorce
Lighting Consultant: Jacques Bobroff
Metalwork: L'Univers d'Aluminium

Leatherwork/Carpets/Tapestry: Domeau &
Pérès
Resins: Sept Résines, Mediterra Design
Sound: SES Giraudon
Hardener: Benôit B

Himmelreich
RheinRuhrZentrum
KARSTADT Arkaden im RRZ Mülheim
Humboldtring 5
45472 Mülheim
Germany
Design: Jordan Mozer and Associates Ltd
320 W. Ohio St, 7th Floor
Chicago, IL 60610
USA
www.mozer.com
Project Team: Jordan Mozer (Principal
Designer), Jeffrey W. Carloss
(Partner/Design Architect), Beverlee Mozer
(Project Manager), Larry Traxler, Bill Ewert
(project designers)
Client: Karstadt
Architecture Firm: Buehl Architects in
collaboration with Soda/Andreus Mueller
and the Karstadt architecture team

Jimmy Woo
Korte Leidsedwarsstraat 18
1017 Amsterdam
The Netherlands
www.jimmywoo.com
Concept and Interior Design: Binc
Interiorstuff and Casper Reinders
Naarderstraat 17
1251 Ax Laren
The Netherlands
www.binc.nl
Client: TAO Group Amsterdam
Owner: Casper Reinders
Main Contractor: Horstermeer
Interiorbuilders
Light Design: Eric Kuster
Light Supplier: Modular Systems
Sound: Function One Systems
Artwork: Marc van Holden and John Breed
(walls and bronze doors)
Furniture: Marac Italy and Roche Bobois
Custom-made fabric and wall-coverings:
Eric Kuster

Kabaret's Prophecy
16–18 Beak Street
London W1F 9RD
UK
www.kabaretsprophecy.com
Interior Architect: David Collins Architecture
and Design
6–7 Chelsea Wharf
Lots Road
London SW10 OQL
UK
www.davidcollins.com

Client: Undisclosed
Consultant (lighting, graphics, a/v, etc): UVA (United Visual Artists)
Bathroom Design: David Collins in collaboration with artist Jamie Hewlett
Floor: Laser cut vinyl by David Collins to a custom design
Wall: LED wall built by Creative Technology, content designed by UVA
Lighting: Verner Panton 'Feature Pendant'
Furniture: custom-designed banquettes by David Collins
Custom-designed Entrance Chandelier: David Collins and Chris Levine with Swarowski Crystal

Kong
1 rue du Pont Neuf
75001 Paris
France
www.kong.fr
Interior Architecture: Philippe Starck
18/20 rue du Faubourg du Temple
75011 Paris
France
www.starck.com
Project team: Philippe Starck, Dorothée Boissier
Client: Laurent Taïb
Project Manager: Frédéric Turpin
Glass work concept: Jean-Jacques Ory
Music: Béatrice Ärdisson
Graphics and Animations: Thibaut Mathieu for CakeDesign and spasmdesign

Le Chlösterli
8783 Grund B
Gstaad
Switzerland
www.chlosterli.com
Interior Design: Agence Patrick Jouin
8 Passage de la Bonne Graine
75011 Paris
France
www.patrickjouin.com
Project Team: Patrick Jouin, Tania Cohen (interior architect); Laurent Janvier (designer), Tomoko Anyoji (architect); Sanjit Manku (architect)
Client: M. Michel Pastor and Mlle Delphine Pastor
Architect: Robert Stutz
Lighting Concept: Hervé Descottes
Lighting: SES Giraudon
Graphics: Philippe David
Wood Fire Video: Souvenirs from the earth
Wooden Terrace and Tables: Michel Poupion
Metalwork: Metalbau Stoller
Woodwork: Gebrüder Blatti Holzbau
Natural Stone Paving: Christian Messerli
Wooden Floor: Müller-Hirschi AG
Wine Celler: Chambrair

The Loft
W 8+9
3 Lime Street
King Street Wharf
Sydney, NSW 2000
Australia

www.theloftsydney.com
Architect: Dale Jones-Evans Pty Ltd Architects
Loft 1
50–54 Ann Street
Surry Hills, NSW 2010
Australia
www.dje.com.au
Project Team: Dale Jones-Evans, Paul Myers, Maki Yamaji, Kathryn Mellander
Client: John Duncan and Fraser Short
Furniture: designed by DJE P/L and manufactured by Club Décor
Chandeliers: designed by DJE P/L and manufactured by Di Emme

Megu
62 Thomas Street
New York, NY 10013
USA
www.megunyc.com
Interior Design: Glamorous Co. Ltd.
Address as before
Project Team: Yasumichi Morita, Satomi Hatanaka, Seiji Sakagami
Client: Koji Imai (Food Scope, New York, Inc.)
Contractor: Kudos Construction Corp.
Lighting Consultant: Kenji Ito
Consultant: Hashimoto & Partners, Inc. (Osamu Hashimoto, Sachiko M. Masaki)
Construction Supervisor: Toshi Enterprise Inc. (Toshihiko Hashimoto)
Furniture: Complex (Lef Inc) – loose chairs; Cmack Construction – custom-made tables

Mountain
473 Gin Ling Way
Chinatown
Los Angeles, CA 90012
USA
www.themountainbar.com
Interior Design: Jorge Pardo Sculpture in collaboration with Mark McManus
5305 Alhambra Avenue
Los Angeles, CA 90032
USA
jps@jorgepardosculpture.com
Client: Jorge Pardo, Steve Hanson, Mark McManus

MYNT
1921 Collins Avenue
Miami Beach, FL
USA
www.myntlounge.com
Interior Design: Arcila-Duque Furniture Interiors, Inc.
4925 Collins Avenue, Suite 10G
Miami Beach, FL 33140
USA
www.arcila-duque.com
Project Team: Juan Carlos Arcila-Duque (designer), Dania Becerra (project manager)
Client: Nicola Siervo, Roberto Caan
Architectural Consultants: Charles Benson

Nectar
Bellagio Resort Hotel
3600 South Las Vegas Blvd
Las Vegas, NV 89109
USA
www.bellagio.com
Interior Design: Jordan Mozer and Associates Ltd.
Address as before
Project Team: Jordan Mozer (Principal Designer), Jeff Carloss (Principal Design Architect), Beverlee Mozer (Principal Project Manager), Jerry Guerts, Bill Ewert (project architects), Andy Susanto (project industrial designer)
Client: MGM/Mirage
Architecture Firm: Atlandia Design in collaboration with Marnell Correo

Opal
36 Gloucester Road
London SW7 4QT
UK
www.etranger.co.uk
Interior Design: Andy Martin Associates
8a All Saints Road
London W11 1HH
UK
www.andymartinassociates.com
Project Team: Andy Martin, Tom Davies, Max de Rosee, Manika Khosla
Client: Ibi Issolah
Structural Engineer: Peter Holliday Associates
Main Contractor: Helix 3D
Rockwork: Helix 3D
Subcontractors: Simon Markey Electrical (electrical); A&K AC (mechanical); Protec (fire); Richardson Re-upholstery (furniture); Chaos (sound); Interbar (bar)

Perbacco
Carrer Sant Gaudenci 5
Sitges (Barcelona) E-08870
Spain
http://per_bacco.eresmas.com
Workcelona
Pau Claris 149 3o 2a
Barcelona E-08009
Spain
www.workcelona.com
Project Team: Stefano Colli and Eugenio Martínez Fons architects
Client: Carlos Roses

Powder
421 West 16th Street
New York, NY
USA
Interior Design: Karim Rashid
357 West 17th Street
New York, NY 10011
USA
www.karimrashid.com
Client: Powder Deep Studios
Lighting: Focus Lighting

Q! Hotel Bar
Knesebeckstr 67
Berlin 10623
Germany
www.q-berlin.de
Designer: Graft
Borsigstrasse 33
Berlin 10115
Germany
www.graftlab.com
Client: Wanzl & Co Bauträgergesellschaft KG
Wave continuous wood/linoleum surfaces: Forbo Flooring – construction by Tischlerei Konrad Fenzi
Furniture: custom design by Graft, constructed by Tischlerei Konrad Fenzi
Bar Stools: 'Lem' manufactured by La Palma
Lounge Chairs: 'Fjord' manufactured by Moroso

Quo
511 W. 28th Street
New York, NY 10018
USA
www.quonyc.com
Interior Design: Dupoux Design
Address as before
Client: Gary Malhorta and Carlo Seneca
General Contractor: Carlo Seneca, C&A Seneca Construction
Audio System: Joe Lodi, Advanced Audio Technology
Lighting: Robert Singer, Robert Singer & Associates Inc.

Red Cat Club
Emmerich-josef-str 13
D-55116 Mainz
Germany
www.redcat-club.de
Interior Design: Timpe + Wendling Architekten
Soderstr 106
D-64287 Darmstadt
Germany
www.timpe-wendling.com
Project Team: Jakob Timpe, Peter Wendling
Client: Simone Schwab, Kai Stolzmann – Red Cat Club
Contractors: Florian Schick (woodwork and carpentry); Alexander Kern (steel, plasterboards); Carsten Rengel (electricity); Beate Steinbronn (fabrics and curtains); Kai Stolzmann (concrete and masonry); Simone Schwab (everything else)

Shochu Lounge
37 Charlotte Street
London W1T 1RR
UK
Interior Design: Super Potato
30-34-17
Kamikitazawa
Setagaya-ku
Tokyo 156-0057
Japan
www.superpotato.jp

Project Team: Noriyoshi Muramatsu,
(5-27-32-502 Minamidai, Nakano-ku, Tokyo
164-0014, Japan)
Client: Rainer Becker and Arjun Waney
Main Contractor: John Nash, Subdale PLC

So-An
3cs Bldg
7F Shinbashi
2-8-9 Minato-ku
Tokyo 105-0004
Japan
http://3cs.co.jp/restaurant/index.html
Interior Design: Zokei Syudan Co. Ltd.
Adress as before
Client: 3CS Hotel & Restaurant Inc.
Contractor: Shiba Sangyou Inc.

Sonotheque
1444 West Chicago
Chicago, IL
USA
www.sonotheque.net
Interior Design: Suhail Design
2041 West Carroll Avenue
Chicago, IL 60612
USA
www.suhail.com
Client: Donald J. Madia, Terry Alexander
and Joe Bryl
Associate Architect: Mhairi McVicar,
James & Kutyla Architects, LLC
Builder: Novelli Design Build
Furniture: Suhail
DJ Booth: Kiehler Design Build
Speaker Installation: Sound Investment
Bar and Floor Installation: Stone Cutters
Graphic Design: Struggle, Inc.

Supperclubcruise
Amsterdam, travelling to different locations
www.supperclubcruise.nl
Designer: Concrete Architectural Associates
Rozengracht 133 III
101 6LV Amsterdam
The Netherlands
www.concrete.archined.nl
Project Team: Gilian Schrofer, Rob
Wagemans, Joris Angevaare, Erik van Dillen
Client: IQ Creative and Healers and Beads
Light and Sound Consultant: Ampco-
Flashlight
Shipbuilding Consultant: F.A. Consultant
Manufacturers: Ubachs Betimmeringen BV
(furniture); H2B Houtbewerking en Interieur
(furniture); Jozef & zv (fixtures and fittings);
Vermeulen Kunststoftoepassingen (floor);
Schouten Plafonds (stretch ceiling); Vasco
Horeca Facilities (lighting and electrical);
Schilderbedrijf Bont (paintworks);
Wijnheumer Metaalbewerking (metal
finishes); Fairies Timmer-en Klussenbedrijf
(metal constructions)

TMSK
Shanghai
China
Interior Design: LorettaYang Hui-Shan
and Chang Yi

c/o Shanghai TMSK Restaurant
Management Co. Ltd.
Unit 2, No. 11, Beili, Xintiandi Square
Lane 181
Taicang Rd
Shanghai
China
Credits not available at time of going to print

UNA Hotel Vittoria Lounge
Via Pisana 59
50143 Florence
Italy
www.unahotels.it
Interior Design: Fabio Novembre
Address as before
Project Team: Fabio Novembre, Carlo
Formisano, Lorenzo de Nicola, Giuseppina
Flor, Ramon Karges
Client: UNA Hotels and Resorts
Main Contractor: Tino Sana srl
General Contractor: C.P.F.
Electricity: Consorzio Artim
Air Conditioning: Gino Battaglini
Floor Covering: Pastellone Veneziano
by Collezioni Ricordi
Special Structures: Loop by Tino Sana
covered with Opus Romano mosaic
by Bisazza
Lighting: Modular, chandelier by Nucleo
Seating: AND Sofa by Fabio Novembre
for Cappellini

Universum Lounge
Kurfürstendamm 153
D-10709 Berlin
Germany
www.universumlounge.de
Interior Architect: Plajer + Franz Studio
Erkelenzdamm 59-61
Berlin 10999
Germany
www.plajer-franz.de
Project Team: Alexander Plajer, Werner
Franz, Birgit Kottenstede, Isabel Albano-
Müller
Client: Franco Francucci
Floor and Wall Contractor: biofarben
Curtain Contractor: hein & objekte
Barfront: fa berndt

ViBE
1, Aristophanous Street
Plareia Iroon (Iroon Square)
Psiri
Athens
Greece
www.vibe.gr
Interior Architect: Dimitris Naoumis
Architect Studies Office
24 Psychari Street
Galatsi 11141
Athens
Greece
Project Team: Dimitris Naoumis; Stelios
Kalogerakis (graphic design)
Client: Grigoris Samourkasoglou

Villa Zévaco
Corner Blvd Franklin Roosevelt-
Alexandre 1er
Casablanca
Morocco
Interior Design: Andy Martin Associates
Adress as before
Project Team: Andy Martin, Tom Davies,
Marco Ortiz, Geraldine Fourmon, Jelal El-Ali,
Darwinda Sidu
Client: Mehdi Bahraoui
Local Architect: Hargam
Lighting Consultant: Kate Wilkins
M&E Consultant: Nombret
Structural Engineer: Tross Ingeniers

Woman
C/ Perpinyà 17
Terassa
Spain
Interior Design: Lola Lago
Balmes No. 5
Bellaterra
08193 Barcelona
Spain
www.lolalagointeriores.com
Client: Cursa 2000 y asociados
Construction: J.O. & M.A. Egara sl
Structural Engineer: Juan Bové & Juan Calaf
Electricity: Instel Terrassa
Illumination: Lumen's Boulevard
Climatization: Antoni Cid sl
Carpentry: Forest sl
Atrezzo: Again
Ceramics: Alicer
Furniture Design: Lola Lago
Graphic Design: Agustín
Lighting Supplier: Sistemas Tecnicos
de Iluminación

XL
357 West 16th Street
New York, NY
USA
www.xlnewyork.com
Architecture, Interiors and Furniture:
Desgrippes Gobé Group
Address as before
Project Team: Sam O'Donahue, Rena
Gyftopolous, Leyden Yaeger, David Ashen
Client: Wonder Works Construction Corp.
Lighting Design: Light Projects
General Contractor: Wonderworks
Construction

Zenzibar Lounge
Ma Dang Lu
Xintiandi
Shanghai
China
Interior Design: AFSO
Unit 2001 Fairmont House
8 Cotton Tree Drive
Central Hong Kong
China
www.afso.com
Project Team: Andre Fu, Benson Lee,
Jackie Hsu, Joanna Chan, Darren Lam
Client: Zen Group

Main Contractor: Lu Dao Construction Ltd
Furniture and Lighting Design: AFSO
Furniture Manufacturer: Lu Dao
Construction Ltd
Fabric Supplier for silk taffeta : Cetec Ltd
Wall Tiles designed by AFSO

Zouk
113 Jalan Ampang
50450 Kuala Lumpur
Malaysia
www.zoukclub.com.ny
Architect: ZDR Studio
5th Floor, Menara Aik Hua
Changkat Raja Chulan, 50200
Kuala Lumpur
Malaysia
www.zd-r.com
Client: Zouk Club (KL) Sdn Bhd,
Interior Design: ZDR in collaboration with
Space Furniture
Main Contractor: Al-Ambia
Structural Engineer: Dereka Structure
Consult
Mechanical and Electrical Engineer: MESC
Engineering
Quantity Surveyor: KPK Quantity Surveyor
Interior Sub-Contractor: SKL Interior

Index

Page numbers in *italics* refer to picture captions

Photo credits

Azrul Kevin Abdullah (152–159); Christian Banfield (32–33); Courtesy Berkeley Hotel (6); Saint Blanquat (12 left); Luc Boegly/Artedia (52, 53 right); Karl Bongartz (20–21); Hiepler Brunier (106–109); John Butlin (78–81); Courtesy Concrete Architectural Associates (90–91); Antony Crolla (11 bottom left and right); Dahlin (132–133); Richard Davies (10 left); Dawn Dickerson and Carmel Naude (9 left); Evon Dion (12 right); Roger Dong (140–141); courtesy Dupoux Design (178–179); Thomas Duval (92–95); Alberto Ferrero (7, 104–105, 122–125); Rômulo Fialdini (150–151); Douglas Reid Fogelsen (146–149); Paul Gosney (68–73); Janos Grapow & Andrea Martiradonna (100–101); Happyliving (86–87); John Horner (46–49, 134–139); Farres Jammel (56–57); Benjamin Kaufmann (96–97); Joe Kesrwani (9 right); Courtesy Kong (53 left); Felix Krebs (116–117); Eric Laignel (10 right, 16–17); Michel Landecy (102–103); Rob Lawson (4); Thomas Loof (40–43); Matteo Piazza (8 left); Courtesy of Andy Martin Associates (84–85); Olivier Martin-Gambier/Artedia; Andrea Martiradonna (8 right, 15); Michael Mundy (13); Nacasa & Partners (28–29, 30–31, 60–67, 74–77, 88–89); Ivan Nemec (114–115); Daniel Nicolas (44–45); Monica Nouwens (24–27); Kirill Ovchinikov (160–167); Eugeni Pons (36–39); Nikos Psihogios (22–23); Matti Pykkö (126–131); Emmanuel Raab (168–177); Tony Robbins (14 bottom); courtesy Shanghai TMSK Restaurant Management Co. Ltd. (82–83); Doug Snower, Chicago (54–55, 58–59); Hugo Thomassen (110–111); Javier Tles (34–35); Meg Turner (11 top); Walter Vandenbrink (118–121); Adrian Wilson (142–145)

Specially commissioned photography on pages 18, 50, 98 and 112 by Fredrika Lökholm and Martin Slivka.

The publishers would like to thank the following for kind permission to photograph in their establishments:

Cocoon Restaurant, Regent Street, London (18)
The Cumberland Hotel, London (50)
Loungelover, London (98)
Shaun + Joe, London (112)

Author's acknowledgements

Thanks to the team at Laurence King Publishing. In particular commissioning editor Philip Cooper for suggesting that we endure this torturous process for the third time, my copy-editor Simon Cowell for his wonderful wit and wisdom, project editor Liz Faber for having the patience of a saint, Kim Sinclair for production, Jennifer Hudson for assisting in the maddening gathering of material and Laura Willis for ensuring that the world knows all about it when the book eventually surfaces.

To my two favourite people, Joan Ryder and Damon Syson, thanks for putting up with me in 'book mode'.

Steve Price of Plan-b Studio, thanks for your design talents. Regarding the cover and chapter divider photography, thanks to Fredrika Lökholm and Martin Slivka, for immediately getting it and ensuring that the book looks so beautiful. For locations, Hassan and the team at Loungelover, Paul Deeming, Sauce Communications and the team at Cocoon, Shaun Clarkson and Shaun + Joe, Jane Moore at the Cumberland Hotel, David Collins, Meena Khera Associates, Annika Stark at UVA and Josie Barlow at Kabarat's Prophecy – thanks, we couldn't have done it without you.

To the buyers of *Bar and Club Design* (Laurence King, 2002) thanks for making the original version successful enough for a sequel – long may your appetite for design books continue.

And finally, to all the architecture and design practices, proprietors, press officers, photographic agents and photographers who have spared their precious time and provided me with the inspiration, information and material that has made this book possible. This book is dedicated to you all, keep 'em coming…